The New Asian Home

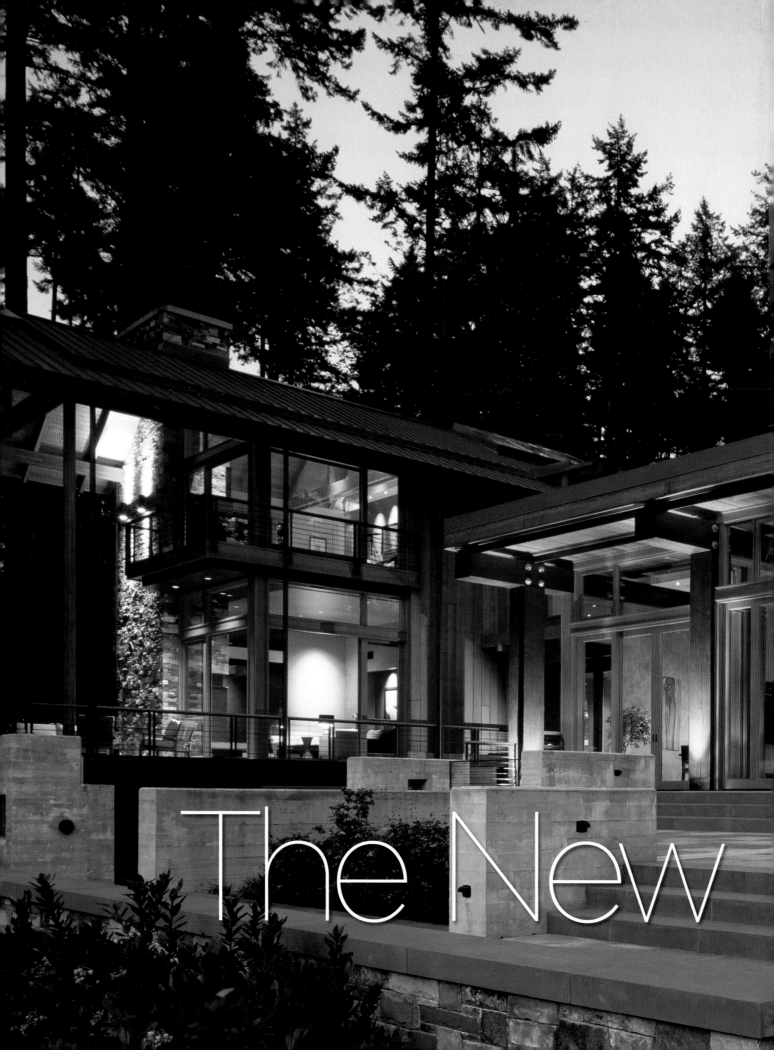

The New

Kendra Langeteig

Asian Home

Gibbs Smith, Publisher
TO ENRICH AND INSPIRE HUMANKIND
Salt Lake City | Charleston | Santa Fe | Santa Barbara

TO THE MEMORY OF MY PARENTS

First Edition
12 11 10 09 08   5 4 3 2 1

Text © 2008 Kendra Langeteig
Photographs © 2008 as noted on page 181

Published by
Gibbs Smith, Publisher
P.O. Box 667
Layton, Utah 84041

Orders: 1.800.835.4993
www.gibbs-smith.com

Designed by Debra McQuiston
Printed and bound in China

Library of Congress Cataloging-in-Publication Data

Langeteig, Kendra.
  The new Asian home / Kendra Langeteig. — 1st ed.
     p. cm.
  Includes bibliographical references.
  ISBN-13: 978-1-4236-0046-6
  ISBN-10: 1-4236-0046-0
  1. Architecture, Domestic—United States—Asian influences. 2.
Architecture, Domestic—Environmental aspects—United States. I. Title.

NA7205.L354 2008
728'.370973—dc22
                              2007043200

ACKNOWLEDGMENTS

The houses featured in this book are built in beautiful private locations—
deep in the woods, on the shore of the ocean, high in the mountains—
special places designed to provide sanctuary from the cares and eyes of the
world. I am grateful to the owners for allowing me to visit their wonderful
homes (if only, in many cases, through pictures and stories) and to share
these inspirational home designs with my readers.

The old saying "A picture is worth a thousand words" holds true here. The
ideas of this book could not be conveyed without the images of its photographers. Architecture, like any art form, must be experienced firsthand to
be truly appreciated. And pictures better describe that experience than I
can explain it in words. I am grateful to the photographers for contributing
the outstanding photographs in this book. Special thanks to Tom Bender,
Bennett Bean, Tony Gwilliam, Maya Lin Studio, Sotheby's, and Peacock &
Lewis, Architects, for permission to use archival photography.

It would be difficult to do justice to the architecture featured in this book
in the space of so few pages. The architects who designed these homes
deserve high praise for their committment to architecture that enriches
the lives of others and serves the needs of the earth. I am grateful to

CONTENTS

INTRODUCTION

8

Traditional Asian houses connect with natural surroundings in ways not traditionally experienced in the West. Conceived as part of the balance of nature, Asian architecture was designed to work in harmony with the earth. More than the product of practical innovations developed in response to climate and resources, and distinct from traditional Western practices, Asian building methods were guided by the principles of ancient design philosophies. The orientation of a house, the selection and placement of a beam, or the design of a roof signified a builder's sacred transactions with the natural world to bring the architecture into balance with the universe. Traditional buildings, from farmhouses to grand pavilions, expressed reverence for nature and a humble appreciation of our place in the greater scheme of things.

Here in the not-so-wise-and-ancient West, architects and designers increasingly look to traditional Asian models for inspiration for the American home as we move into the twenty-first century. Introducing Asian design elements can make the home a peaceful sanctuary from the hectic tempo of contemporary life. Beyond the widespread use of materials such as bamboo for a more natural aesthetic, classic Asian design principles—balance, harmony, simplicity, and transparency between indoor and outdoor space—have entered the design vocabulary. In a matter of decades, the American house

has transformed from a structure conceived with a set floor plan and standardized building methods and materials to a more flexible open space with revealed structural elements and natural materials integrated with the site. The shift toward a holistic "Asian" perspective is a healthy sign of change. It affirms the new paradigm that recognizes the connection between all living beings, a view that promotes respect for the environment and encourages us to take better care of the earth and ourselves in the way we build our homes.

Featured in this book are twenty-three designs that represent some of the most interesting and important examples of Asian influence in the new ecology of American home design. As the diverse selection illustrates, "New Asian" refers not to one but many traditional Asian styles and influences given exciting new interpretations in American homes. Some of these designs have a distinct Asian character, with aesthetic elements directly drawn from traditional models. Other homes more subtly evoke a fusion with Asian aesthetics, often designed for clients with Asian and modern sensibilities who wanted a serene contemporary home with refreshing novelty. The projects range from handcrafted traditional structures to spectacular custom designs featuring new technology and regional vernacular to affordable modular houses built with eco-friendly kit-systems components. These innovative projects represent the work of architects and designers who like to think outside the box of Western tradition: pioneers in environmental design, artists, master craftsmen—visionary thinkers committed to architecture that is good for the earth, bringing peace and well-being to those who live in its space.

The book is arranged in six chapters that highlight some of the main themes explored in the development of the new Asian home.

JOINING TRADITIONS: This opening chapter features original interpretations of classic Japanese architecture. It includes examples of the exquisite craftsmanship of Len Brackett of East Wind, Inc., and Hiroshi Sakaguchi of Ki Arts, master carpenters trained in the art of Japanese joinery who give the tradition new life in the West. Featured are two residential projects and a teahouse garden complex located in California. The Japanese folk house inspired architect Michael Fuller's design for an elegant mountain retreat that gives classic folk house elements an Arts and Crafts refinement. Richard Van Den Berg translates authentic folk house design to a contemporary house on Lake Michigan.

DIRECTIONS FROM THE NATURAL HOUSE: Frank Lloyd Wright's "natural house" philosophy moves into the twenty-first century in the imaginative designs featured in this chapter. John Randal McDonald gives Wright's organic architecture a modernist revision with Buddhist temple character in a home designed for collectors of George Nakashima furniture. Tommy Hein's design for a mountain retreat fuses Wright's vocabulary with Taoist philosophy and Japanese design, and references the Ise Shrine and Southwest monuments. Wright's masterpiece Fallingwater inspired architect Joseph Lancor's romantic design for a house with a Tibetan monastery theme set in tropical paradise.

THE NATURE OF PLACE: This chapter features projects by environmental designers who build houses with nature foremost in mind. Attention to regional vernacular, local materials, and intuitive site-sensitive design solutions characterize this work. Two house designs on the Oregon Coast illustrate the wizardry of architect Tom Bender, who introduced feng shui to America. A clean modernist economy and structural expressiveness that parallel the Japanese aesthetic characterize the Hawaiian home designed by architect Jim Cutler. Architect Philip Beck's design for a Mount Rainier pavilion demonstrates ingenious application of new technology for a seamless connection with nature. Also featured is an organic tropical design by architectural designer Carey Smoot, who championed the return of native tropical vernacular in Hawaii.

SHIFTING CONTEXTS: This chapter takes a look at two home renovations that playfully shift traditional Western house designs toward the East: an eighteenth-century New Jersey farmhouse and an island-ranch home in Florida are converted into hybrid designs with a multicultural Asian edge. Artist Bennett Bean's modernist design for an addition to his farmhouse illustrates how merging different traditions can create fluid spatial and cultural boundaries. Jon Olson, of Peacock & Lewis, Architects, in collaboration with his clients, transformed a Florida home into an exuberant contemporary hybrid with Balinese character.

DESIGNS ON THE BOUNDARIES: This chapter features cutting-edge designs by four modernists whose work is neither East nor West but somewhere in between: Maya Lin, Jim Cutler of Cutler Anderson, Architects, Craig Curtis of the Miller/Hull Partnership, and Shigeru Ban. Their vibrant architecture emphasizes economy, clarity, dissolution of spatial boundaries, and experimentation with new materials

and technology for sustainable design solutions. The featured projects are distinguished by wit and resourcefulness: an urban duplex with shape-shifting components, a Napa Valley estate built with rammed-earth material, an island residence in Puget Sound built with timbers salvaged from a sunken ship, and a "Furniture House" built entirely with prefabricated furniture modules.

HOUSES TO GO: The final chapter features Asian-inspired modular houses that are rewriting the definition of "kit" houses with their flexible construction and low-impact ecological design. Architect Tony Gwilliam developed an eco-friendly prototype based on Balinese and Japanese design: the T-House. Carey Smoot, another designer inspired by indigenous tropical vernacular, modeled the Minahasa House after the houses of North Sulawesi. Haiku Houses, offers a modular systems-built version of the sixteenth-century Japanese country house. (Artist John Hersey gives the Haiku House product a modernist interpretation.) Master carpenter Paul Discoe developed a prototype called Rikyu that fuses traditional Asian joinery with Western technology for a low-budget, sustainable home. The first two houses built by his company are featured here.

It took my breath away. . . . Until that day, I had never been interested in architectural space. It was almost as if one could see the air enclosed by the building, could almost touch it—something like the way one can see the air outside on a damp cool morning. . . . Space becomes something positive; it isn't just empty, it's really *there*. Wouldn't it be amazing, I thought, to be able to build such sublime spaces?

—Len Brackett

This spa-like bath design, with
Japanese soak tub, pebbled
flooring, and atmospheric light,
encourages a tranquil mood.

JOINING TRADITIONS: THE JAPANESE HOUSE IN THE WEST

THE ZEN SPACE OF
JAPANESE ARCHITECTURE

BRACKETT RESIDENCE

LOCATION: NEVADA CITY, CALIFORNIA **DESIGNER:** LEN BRACKETT, EAST WIND, INC.

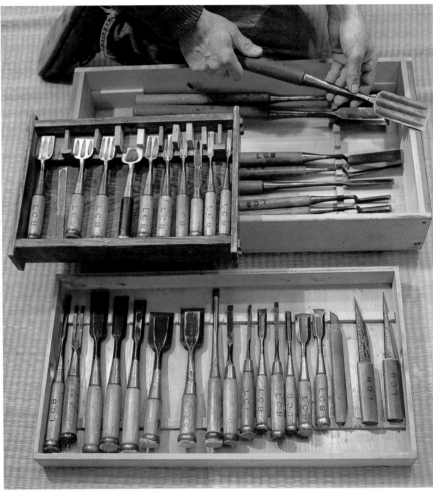

ABOVE: The Brackett residence is modeled after the elegant residential style of the Taisho period (1912–1926). The design incorporates elements of the temple architecture Brackett studied during his carpentry apprenticeship in Japan.

ABOVE RIGHT: Brackett displays his treasured Japanese joinery tools.

There are certain Westerners whose first exposure to the simple elegance of traditional Japanese architecture strikes a deep chord. Len Brackett, owner of East Wind, Inc., a northern California company specializing in Japanese architecture, design, and woodworking, experienced this kind of epiphany when he entered a thirteenth-century Zen Buddhist temple in Kyoto, Japan, for the first time.

Brackett was so moved by the experience that he returned to Japan (after completing a degree in Asian studies) to learn the language and find out "how Japan worked." He then ventured on an arduous five-year, eighty-hour-week apprenticeship in Japanese temple carpentry at the Daitokuji sub-temple complex in Kyoto under a master carpenter. Returning to America in 1976, Brackett started an architectural design firm whose approach went directly against the mainstream building trend. While construction companies were cranking out fast-built standardized houses in plywood and particleboard, East Wind began slowly producing handcrafted Japanese timber-frame houses in the finest woods designed to last 200 years.

18 At a time when the traditional Japanese house has all but disappeared in Japan, through the Westernization of the culture and the widespread development of modern building methods and materials, Brackett plays an important (if ironic) role in keeping the tradition alive by adapting its vernacular forms to an American context. East Wind specializes in a Western hybrid based on authentic Japanese designs, a "mixed bag" of stylistic influences, ranging from temple architecture to Alpine farmhouses. The company has crafted architecture for some notable Western clients. Richard Baker, *roshi* (heir to Shunryu Suzuki, who brought Zen Buddhism to San Francisco), commissioned Brackett to build structures at Crestone Mountain Zen Center in Crestone, Colorado. East Wind built the gates and bridges for Oracle founder Larry Ellison's Japanese-themed estate in Woodside, California.

East Wind continues to maintain high standards in the selection of quality material, even in a time of shrinking forests and endangered species of wood, and has been resourceful in working with recycled materials. Since his early days building Japanese houses on the West Coast, Brackett has developed ways to modify traditional elements to suit the Western lifestyle preferences of his American clients. In the process, Brackett has created what he terms a "whole new kind of architecture," representing a happy fusion between Japanese design principles and Western building practices.

FACING: Rooms facing the inside corridor, partitioned by *shoji* (screens), transition to the viewing garden in the courtyard.

RIGHT: The *irori* (sunken hearth) in the dining area is a classic feature of the Japanese folk house.

When Brackett returned to California in 1976, fresh from his apprenticeship in Japanese temple carpentry in Kyoto, he immediately set to work building a Japanese house for his family on twenty secluded acres in the foothills of the Sierra Nevada. Brackett built this first house (where he lived for more than thirty years) with the help of his friend and lifelong apprentice, Walter Hardzog. The architecture is modeled after the elegant residential style of the Taisho period (1912–1926). The timber-frame structure was crafted from 5,000 board feet of the finest cedars (Port Orford, red, and incense) and sugar pine. The entire process—from designing the layout, selecting the wood, and cutting and hand planing the components to assembling the post-and-beam structure, roofing, and plastering—took four years. "All hand work," explains Brackett. "None of the machinery we have today to speed the process." This project served as the point of departure for East Wind, the Japanese architecture and woodworking company Brackett founded on the property beginning with a small shop that expanded to a 4,500-square-foot shop, an office, and two acres covered with thirty species of dry lumber.

Designing his first house, Brackett reproduced classic features of the traditional Japanese *hirya* (wide house), a residential style that sprawls over the site. This early hybrid incorporates elements of the temple architecture Brackett knew intimately from his carpentry training in Japan—gracefully

ABOVE LEFT: The windows over the cedar soaking tub, *ofuso*, in the bath are carefully positioned to give the bather a tranquil forest view.

LEFT: A traditional round window with bamboo lattices brings soft diffused light into the room.

FACING: Without the clutter and distraction of furnishings, as in Western décor, attention is drawn to the beauty of the lustrous, fragrant woods and forest views.

carved beams, central courtyard garden, white-painted rafter tips (now an East Wind signature), and distinctive roof structures. Poet Gary Snyder, friend and neighbor in Brackett's "back to the land" community, referred to the grand style of the house as *"Sumitomo besso,"* meaning the kind of house the Sumitomos, a wealthy family in ancient Japan, would build for themselves as a country retreat.

Although grand in scheme by Japanese standards, the architecture is hardly grand in scale by comparison with Western houses. In the 2,000-square-foot house plan, a modest 850 square feet comprise the main living areas—living-dining area, study, bath, and flexible space that can be configured into as many as six bedrooms with *shoji* (sliding screens). The wood verandas, or *engawa*, wrapping the exterior of the house beneath the eaves, and the interior corridors and central courtyard garden consume most of the footprint. The house is about fifty-five *tsubo*, the traditional area measure of Japanese houses,

based on a module called a *ken* (about 3 x 6 feet, the size of a *tatami* mat). The large amount of architecture devoted to transitional space between house and garden highlights the central importance of nature in Japanese design. Brackett emphasizes the need for a Japanese house to be "connected to what's happening outside in the natural world," even in cold, snowy alpine regions of Japan similar in character to this San Juan ridge site. For a seamless interface with nature, Brackett creates "soft transitions"

between exterior and interior space with the engawa.

To negotiate the transitional space of the Brackett house, one enters through the *genkan* (entry), located under the main roof, and steps up eighteen inches on the "step-up board" to the wood floor of the interior corridor that opens to a central open-roofed courtyard garden. Shoji on the interior and sliding glass doors on the exterior serve to open the house to the outdoors and provide a flexible and ever-changing

relationship with the natural environment. The traditional wooden shutters and blinds can be drawn during inclement weather.

Immaterial elements of light and shadow are as important to Japanese design as its material elements. Shoji serve the aesthetic function of framing views and controlling the quality of light. Following traditional Japanese style, the few fixed windows of the Brackett house are set low to provide views from a seated position. Placement and scale are important.

In this design, round windows with bamboo lattices set in mud-plaster walls emit soft diffused light.

The Brackett house was built as an experiment for living in the old style of sixteenth-century Japan, where it was customary to fire up the wood-stove for a bath, and sleep on a futon. Brackett and his houses, however, have changed with the times. "Today I'd rather be more comfortable, since I don't think Western modifications necessitate degrading the proportions of beauty in the original form."

HIDE AND REVEAL: THE ART OF SURPRISE IN JAPANESE DESIGN

PRIVATE RESIDENCE

LOCATION: TIBURON, CALIFORNIA **ARCHITECT:** LEN BRACKETT, EAST WIND, INC.

ABOVE: The Tiburon architecture draws inspiration from *sukiya* style, a sophisticated blend of rusticity and refinement that owes much to Japanese teahouse and garden design.

ABOVE RIGHT: In the main living area, Brackett substituted the *engawa* (veranda) of traditional Japanese house design for seated window bays.

With its mild Pacific climate, hardwood forests, and history of Asian settlement, the San Francisco Bay Area is an especially congenial location for the traditional Japanese timber-frame houses produced by East Wind. The company's first major residential project, and Len Brackett's "first shot at a Westernized version of the Japanese house," was a spec house in Tiburon, California, completed in 1986. The renovation of this house nearly twenty years later by its second owners represents East Wind's most significant project in the development of Japanese archi-

tecture for a Western client. The subtly refined architecture, nestled into an acre of landscaped gardens on a steep site overlooking San Francisco Bay, is a virtual handbook in Japanese design given a Western spin.

The architecture incorporates classic elements of *sukiya* style, a refined seventeenth-century aesthetic with natural elements of teahouse architecture, such as mud walls and reed windows, most of which date from the original East Wind design. When the house changed hands in 2000, the purchase was contingent

LEFT: The formal entry of the residence affords a glimpse through many layers of architectural space.

FACING: To connect the garden to the back of the house, East Wind built a stunning thirty-foot-long covered walkway with three roof levels and interlocking copper shingles.

upon having East Wind renovate the new owners' home. The original house was designed to accommodate furniture by raising the level of the traditional window height for the changed perspective. Other Western modifications included the substitution of a traditional *engawa* (wood veranda) in the main living area for seated window bays—a design option that has become an East Wind trademark. Revisiting the Tiburon project, Brackett brought two decades of

experience in developing such refinements without sacrificing classic scale and proportion.

East Wind completed the renovations in three phases over a five-year period. The first phase included redesigning the kitchen, renovating all the bathrooms, and adding a 17 x 30-foot elevated deck off the master bedroom. Phase two involved building a traditional *mon* (entrance gate) and plaster wall for an enclosed garden outside the main entrance

of the residence, converting the old garage into a nine-tatami-mat meditation room, and building a detached garage with a covered walkway connection to the house. Jim Pyle, owner of Wu' Way Landscape (Grass Valley, California), a close friend of Brackett, designed both Japanese gardens. To connect the back of the garden to the back of the house, East Wind built a stunning thirty-foot-long covered walkway with three roof levels and interlocking copper shingles.

The third phase of the Tiburon project presented a more daunting challenge: the construction of a 2,000-square-foot addition. "The major design challenge was to integrate the new addition with a view of San Francisco Bay without occluding the existing view," says Brackett. The new building, sited below the main house, features a guest bedroom and bath, a master suite with bath, a large walk-in closet, a general storage area, a kitchenette, and an adjoining interior dry garden. East Wind also built a 16 x 35-foot engawa the length of the new building facing the water, and added an "invisible" three-car garage with grated windows and mud-plaster walls to blend with the original house. "I didn't want it to register as a garage," explains Brackett. "So I plastered the roll-up doors and disguised it as a 'normal building.'" Upgraded amenities, from blackout screens to zone heating, were also discreetly concealed to maintain the traditional Japanese character of the home.

For Brackett, the pleasure in developing this complex architecture for his clients was the opportunity it gave him to explore interesting and exciting design possibilities. "Good architecture is not predictable," observes Brackett. "It surprises, and creates an exciting experience." That element of surprise is difficult to achieve in small-scale designs with fewer twists and turns in the

LEFT: This dramatic rounded window provides an exciting contrast to the rectilinear geometry of gridded screens and post-and-beam elements.

FACING: A meditation room with *tokonoma* (display alcove) and cherry-wood *engawa* (wood veranda) transitions to the pond garden.

plot. In small traditional Japanese houses, the natural materials and exquisite craftsmanship must tell the story. The Tiburon architecture draws inspiration from sukiya style, a sophisticated blend of rusticity and refinement that owes much to the ceremonial teahouse and the "hide and reveal" principle of Japanese garden design. In classic teahouse garden design, the teahouse is approached gradually through a sequence of visual events

that unfolds along the "dewy path." The gradual presentation of views strategically framed by the designer encourages a slower pace to contemplate their aesthetic subtlety, and encourages a sense of discovery and pleasurable surprise.

Many such revelations unfold in the Tiburon residence as you move through the exciting architecture of the new addition. From the upper deck of the main residence, for example, you descend a granite

stairway to access the new wing on the lower level. Coming through a wall of sliding glass doors, you step onto a balcony with a temple-style railing. Directly ahead, a stunning round window, six feet in diameter, glows moonlike through the rails. Brackett explains that this window isn't really round but was inspired by a fluke of nature, an optical illusion. "It's slightly squashed, the way the sun squashes when it sets or rises over the sea."

Five feet below the balcony and down a small staircase, quite unexpectedly, an interior dry garden with an open-roof structure suddenly materializes. Brackett built a *hinoki* (cypress) engawa about eighteen inches above the garden, which is below floor level with large stones, raked gravel, and plants. The "rising sun" window overlooking this garden is fitted with a sliding screen to afford privacy as well as provide views of the garden that can be enjoyed from the master bedroom.

As you walk through the architectural layers of the Tiburon residence, noticing one striking element of the design after another, one view suddenly framing another, the experience is ever changing. The art of surprise in Japanese design, based on a fluid poetic concept of movement through space, is eloquently expressed in this East Wind architecture.

LEFT: The partially opened *shoji* (screen) designed for this oversized window provocatively frames the master bedroom.

ABOVE: This 12 x 12-foot dry garden creates a miniature, otherworldly landscape in the home's interior. The garden was designed as a symbolic space for meditation and viewing. Here, the gravel pattern and rock forms represent flowing water and islands.

MEANWHILE, LET US HAVE A SIP OF TEA …

CARLSTON TEAHOUSE GARDEN COMPLEX

LOCATION: SAN RAFAEL, CALIFORNIA **DESIGNER:** HIROSHI SAKAGUCHI, KI ARTS

The afternoon glow is brightening the bamboos, the fountains are bubbling with delight, the soughing of the pines is heard in our kettle. Let us dream of evanescence, and linger in the beautiful foolishness of things.

—Okakura Kakuzo, *The Book of Tea*

ABOVE: Inside the gate, a beautifully scenic garden path leads to the teahouse.

ABOVE RIGHT: The traditional entrance gate is made of white cedar with a roof of layered red cedar shingles and Japanese ceramic tiles.

Hiroshi Sakaguchi, founder of Ki Arts (1985), a traditional Japanese woodworking company in northern California, is a master carpenter from a family of woodworkers that goes back several generations. Sakaguchi grew up on the Kii Peninsula in Japan, an area known for its beautiful cedar forests—the prized wood of Japanese teahouse and temple carpenters. After years of training in the complex art of joinery construction, a system of building that connects wood by intricate joints rather than screws or nails, Sakaguchi brought his exceptional talents to the United

States. Beginning with an elegant *sukiya*-style house with tearoom at Green Gulch Farm and Retreat Center in Muir Beach (a Buddhist community established by the San Francisco Zen Center), Sakaguchi went on to craft exquisite Japanese garden structures, rooms, and furniture for clients in northern California. Sakaguchi's distinguished work can be found in private residences, public parks, restaurants, and Buddhist temples in Japan, Europe, and Canada, as well as in the United States.

This garden complex in San Rafael, California, designed for Doug and Tomi

Carlston, features the classic architecture of a traditional Japanese teahouse garden: *mon* (entrance gate), *hashi* (bridge), sheltered bench or "waiting building," and teahouse (*chashitsu: cha*, "tea" + *shitsu*, "house"). Several years before Sakaguchi built these teahouse garden structures, the Carlstons had cleared out a large blackberry patch on their property to make room for the rock and water garden. Myogen Steve Stucky, Abbot of the San Francisco Zen Center, designed this classic Japanese garden for the Carlstons—a perfect setting for the jewel of a teahouse created by Sakaguchi.

The elegant style of the Carlston teahouse dates from the Momoyama period when teahouse architecture was influenced by Zen Buddhist temple carpentry and ceremonial tearooms. The style predates the more rustic teahouse later popularized by wealthy shoguns in Japan. During the "cult of tea," *wabi-sabi* (simple, rural) charms were elevated to an art and tea masters transformed the simple custom of drinking tea into a ritualized ceremony, *chanoyu* (tea with water). Because of their reverence for nature, both Buddhist monks and philosophers of teaism appreciated organic idiosyncrasies such as knots in wood and twisted limbs in teahouse architecture.

The Carlston teahouse design has a deceptively simple appearance. In reality, the post-and-beam joinery for

FACING FAR LEFT: The elegant style of the Carlston teahouse, influenced by temple architecture, dates from the Momoyama period.

LEFT: For this *kirizuma* (ridge-roof) style of teahouse, the roof requires multiple layers of cedar shingles.

RIGHT: The eaves of the Carlston teahouse are eleven shingles thick.

a teahouse structure of this quality requires years of training because a perfect fit must be achieved that also preserves the integrity of the natural materials—no easy task. Sakaguchi pointed out that the *engawa* (wood veranda) beams in this teahouse are naturally round and irregular (due to the tree selected for their creation), which makes it especially difficult to get a clean joinery fit. Traditionally, teahouse posts are set at the base in granite stone, and both the hole

in the stone and post joinery must be expertly cut to position the post correctly. For this *kirizuma* (ridge-roof) style of teahouse, inspired by temple architecture, the roof requires multiple layers of cedar shingles. The eaves of the Carlston teahouse are eleven shingles thick. To complete the roof design, Sakaguchi laid imported Japanese ceramic tiles at the ridge top.

Sakaguchi used great precision for crafting every detail of the teahouse architecture. Doug Carlston experi-

enced, firsthand, the care that went into its creation:

Watching the construction was a marvelous experience. As Hiroshi built each element, we saw unfold for us not just the finished work but the layers and layers of detail that went into the smallest elements. Much of this detail isn't even visible in the finished structure—it's just part of the "right" way to do things. I have never seen construction, even of fine furniture, with this kind of care and attention to detail.

33

Measurements for the various components of Japanese architecture are determined from rules passed down by carpenters through the centuries. Teahouse size corresponds to the number of tatami mats (based on a human scale, one tatami is approximately 3 x 6 feet). The Carlston teahouse is a 4.5-mat size—designed to comfortably seat four people for tea. Sakaguchi followed specific proportions for the length, width, and height of the main room, engawa, and traditional teahouse features—*tokonoma* (display alcove) and *mizuya* (a chest or cupboard equipped with utensils for the tea ceremony and ceramic tea bowls). The tearoom's disciplined proportions combined with the simple geometric patterns of *shoji* (wood-framed paper screens), made by Sakaguchi, and tatami balance the natural curves and textures of the woods to create a wonderfully calming environment.

Japanese garden architecture is traditionally designed to showcase the natural character of the woods selected for its construction. "When I make a gate, bridge, pavilion, or any structure for the garden, I must consider not just what the structure looks like now but how nature will age it over time," explains Sakaguchi. All of the wood surfaces, except for the white cedar posts and beams and red cedar shingles, were hand planed to give the wood a lustrous, silky sheen.

As the teahouse ages, these untreated woods will acquire a subtle natural patina to heighten the architecture's grace and beauty.

The exquisite beauty of this teahouse owes much to its luxuriant garden setting. From its intimate interior, the teahouse enjoys delightful views of the koi pond and cascading waterfall below the veranda. Sliding shoji and wooden shutters provide differently framed garden views and varying degrees of privacy as well as shelter from inclement weather. Although the Carlstons seldom have proper tea ceremonies, they use their teahouse throughout most of the year as a quiet and peaceful place to relax, often with small groups of friends. "It is a place to go to explore beauty and to let that beauty work on one when the need arises," says Carlston. "Everyone needs this, and we are extraordinarily lucky to have this gift so close at hand."

ABOVE LEFT: Sliding *shoji* (screens) and wooden blinds crafted by Sakaguchi provide shade and privacy.

ABOVE: The exquisitely crafted *mizuya* (cupboard) is equipped with utensils for the tea ceremony.

ARTS AND CRAFTS FOLK HOUSE

PRIVATE RESIDENCE

LOCATION: TELLURIDE, COLORADO **ARCHITECT:** MICHAEL FULLER ARCHITECTS WITH ANDREA JOVINE, DESIGNER

ABOVE: Michael Fuller's design incorporates the gabled roof of the classic *minka* (Japanese folk house), modified to a less dramatic pitch, for the central structure of the house.

ABOVE RIGHT: The gong-and-gate structure confers a ceremonial note of dignity while winking at the home's merged architectural traditions—Far East and Wild West.

The mountain-home portfolio of Aspen architect Michael Fuller includes some fascinating variations on the Western timber-frame theme in Telluride, Colorado. Among the more elegant is the mountain retreat Fuller designed for a New York couple on a dramatic site overlooking the San Sophia Ridge. The architecture draws inspiration from a timber-frame tradition that precedes its development on the American frontier by centuries: the Japanese folk house, or *minka*. The minka dwellings, reaching the height of their evolution during the Edo period (1600–1868),

were built by master carpenters in alpine regions with heavy snow loads such as found in the Rocky Mountains. As Fuller observes of these parallel traditions: "The same design problem, with 150 years of development in the West, had centuries of refinement in Japan." The Japanese folk house is noted for the rustic beauty of its steep thatched roof that seems to grow out of the landscape, the handcrafted joinery of its wide columns and beams, and its high ceilings. Fuller further explains, "We drew from that tradition to produce a structure similar to the folk house but with a more

refined aesthetic." Taking the minka design in the direction of an Arts and Crafts refinement, Fuller elevates the rustic to the luxurious.

Without re-creating the minka, the architecture attempts to produce the scale and feeling of the Japanese folk house in its structural elements. Fuller's design incorporates the gabled roof of the classic minka, modified to a less dramatic pitch, for the central structure of the house. The design substitutes the traditional mountain-lodge "great room" for the

spacious but more intimate *hiroma* (large high-ceiling living room)—the heart of the Japanese folk house. This open living space forms the central component of the architecture, and flows laterally into two (two-storied) pavilions: stepping up to a dining area, kitchen-family room and guest-room wing; and stepping down to a study, master suite, and lower-level guest-room complex. The architecture steps down the hill to follow the natural slope of the site. The thatched roof typical of the minka is traded for slate

shingles. Cedar shingles cladding the exterior and the native stacked stone featured in the walls and pillars add to the home's rustic character.

The antique gong and *torii* gate structure placed prominently in front of the house and visible from the long approach of the driveway sets the tone for the architecture. It serves as "a nice announcement," says Fuller. This feature represents a creative feng shui solution to a design problem noted by the clients: "The energy coming straight up the

LEFT: Antique Chinese ironwood screens flank the entrance from the foyer to the great room.

RIGHT: Joinery construction finds still-greater refinement with inspired Arts and Crafts detailing. This sculptural skylight illuminates the corridor between foyer and *minka* room.

driveway was diverted by the torii gate and gong structure, causing it to flow around both sides but not blocking it completely." The feature also honors the distinctively Asian spirit of the home. Torii gates, traditionally placed at the entrance of a Buddhist temple or Shinto shrine, mark the boundary between the sacred precincts and the everyday world outside. In the context of the home's western locale, a ranch gate also comes to mind. The gong and gate confer a ceremonial note of dignity while winking at the home's

merged architectural traditions—Far East and Wild West.

For the minka architecture, Fuller incorporated traditional Japanese joinery elements, materials, and construction. The twenty-four-inch posts serving as the main supports, in limited-harvest Port Orford cedar, were purchased from a Canadian lumber company. (These massive posts were originally destined for a Japanese temple project.) All of the joinery was completed on-site, under the direction of master woodworker

Ed Schurer, from the careful selection, measurement, and cutting of the wood to hand-planing the timbers to a satin-smooth finish. Schurer and his crew tried to capture the feeling of an old Japanese farmhouse by keeping the wood close to its natural state. While retaining many classic minka elements, such as the distinctive curved *hari* beams, Fuller eliminated the central pillar and traded the *irori* (sunken central hearth) for a Western-style fireplace. The fireplace was crafted in granite salvaged from

LEFT: The fireplace was crafted in granite salvaged from a village lost to the Three Gorges Dam project on the Yangtze River in China. The owner's mother painted the landscape scene.

FACING: Michael Fuller's design substitutes the traditional mountain-lodge "great room" for the spacious but more intimate *hiroma* (large high-ceiling living room)—the heart of the Japanese folk house.

a village lost to the Three Gorges Dam project on the Yangtze River in China. As Fuller observes of this history, "We made the fire surround from a door threshold that had been stepped over for generations."

The Fuller project in Telluride marked Andrea Jovine's transition from the world of fashion to home interiors. In developing her elegant design concept, Jovine honored the central role of the home's distinctive architectural aesthetic: "It was important that the architecture took center stage. The

material that was used throughout the house, along with the superb craftsmanship, made me mindful to keep a restrained hand with the décor."

Working closely with Fuller and the clients, Jovine created interiors to reflect the integrity and honesty of the materials, both inside and out. "We wanted an understated sophistication that was warm and inviting," explains Jovine. To achieve that warmth and subtlety, Jovine selected a palette of primarily golden tones, "like a warm fire burning." The

gold chromatics of wall pigments and fabrics enhance the natural wood tones of the architecture and radiate a harmonious light, serene and calming in its effect. Jovine's orchestration of contrasting forms and textures creates some of this magic. Juxtapositions between "light and dark, smooth and rough, refined and rustic" are at play, as in the great room, where the post-and-beam structure and stone fireplace balance the clean modernist lines and refined textures of the furniture.

FACING FAR LEFT: Immaterial elements of light and shadow are important to classic Asian design.

FACING LEFT: To create a spa-like environment, Fuller designed an elevated platform for the Japanese soak tub. The pebbled flooring is reminiscent of the Japanese garden. Atmospheric light filters through frosted glass and skylights to encourage a tranquil mood.

RIGHT: To bring light and mountain views into the master bedroom, Jovine designed a floating platform bed with an openwork headboard that doubles as a partition. The delicate painted screen dates from the Edo period.

The extensive Asian art collection of the owners, one of whom is of Chinese descent, inspired the predominantly Asian aesthetic in the design elements. Antique Chinese ironwood screens on sliding tracks elegantly separate the foyer from the great room. Throughout the home, Chinese landscape paintings and Japanese screens depicting classic nature themes—mountains, lakes, birds, and flowers—convey the mood of serenity and contemplation cultivated by Asian artists. Jovine's intuitive selection of fabrics in muted golds and greens harmonize with the antique gold tones of the delicately painted screens. This quiet tonality is effectively countered with bold calligraphic paintings and red accents in the décor that speak to the owners' love of red—a color that symbolizes good fortune to the Chinese.

An Asian theme is carried into the master suite, where a floating platform bed with a Japanese-inspired headboard doubles as a screen-like partition to bring in light and mountain views. Open-work geometry also characterizes the master bath design. To create a spa-like environment, Fuller designed an elevated platform with a Japanese soak tub. Pebbled flooring reminiscent of the Japanese garden, and atmospheric light filtering through *shoji*-screened skylights and frosted glass encourage a sense of calmness and well-being. That peaceful mood resonates through every element of this exquisitely crafted home to create a wonderfully tranquil mountain sanctuary.

THE WAY TO MATSU: FROM KYOTO TO CEDAR GROVE

VAN DEN BERG RESIDENCE

LOCATION: CEDAR GROVE, WISCONSIN **DESIGNERS:** RICHARD AND LILLIAN VAN DEN BERG

Country Matsu by Richard Van Den Berg.

The sign reads: 松寿庵

ABOVE: The house is rooted to its natural surroundings in true Japanese style.

ABOVE RIGHT: The natural-aged cedar post that flanks the entrance was a serendipitous find—a salvaged telephone pole "weathered in Wisconsin air."

BELOW RIGHT: *Country Matsu* by Richard Van Den Berg. An accomplished artist, he rendered this pen-and-ink drawing of his house design.

At the entrance of this woodsy retreat on the shores of Lake Michigan, the Japanese salutation—*Matsu*—greets the visitor. The characters on the sign, which translate to "pine," celebrate the rustic spirit of the architecture and its link with Japanese tradition. The sign was specially made for Dick and Lillian Van Den Berg by a friend in Kyoto to honor the completion of this house designed to replace the home they lost in a catastrophic fire. Country Matsu rose directly over the foundation of the original house built on this lakefront property near Cedar

Grove, a small farming town north of Milwaukee, Wisconsin—worlds apart from the Japanese tradition that inspired this contemporary country house.

When the Van Den Bergs purchased the property, the original house on the site was a log structure with pointed timbers standing fortress-like above the dunes. To convert "the Stockade," as they called it, into a more contemporary week-end retreat, they sawed off the points, painted the camp-brown exterior a cool lavender, cut out a window to frame a big lake view, added a studio onto the master

bedroom, and wrapped an *engawa* (wood veranda) around the front. Japanese kites, prints, and ceramics collected in their travels to Japan and San Francisco, along with a pair of George Nakashima chairs purchased at the Nakashima Studio in New Hope, Pennsylvania, shifted the spirit of the home to the Far East. When the house burned in 1978, most of that history was lost. Only the standing solid-copper hood in the center of the house and salvageable lumber and furniture survived. Dick and Lillian turned the loss into an opportunity to build a house with a more authentic Japanese character.

Dick Van Den Berg, an authority on packaging design and marketing, set to work designing his own version of the Japanese country house. Van Den Berg's hybrid design was drawn from historical research of Japanese architecture, especially the Japanese folk house beloved by architectural historian Teiji Itoh. "It was the character of that house I was trying to capture," Dick explains. Dick and Lillian made several trips to northern California to research residential projects. "In our search for the Japanese contemporary rustic in Pacific Heights, Monterey, we came across a house of Asian design with an open-ceiling scissor roof," explains Dick. That design concept provided a key piece of the puzzle. The "floating" roof has no weight-bearing walls and thus opens up the interior space.

46

The house features an open plan on the first level, with living, dining, and kitchen areas defined by brick partitions. The master suite is privately situated up three steps from the main level. The lower level includes a guest room, sauna (with Japanese-style soak tub), and a 10 x 30-foot design studio. Materials salvaged from the fire inspired key elements of the design. The standing copper hood figures as a central component. The entire downstairs level—including *tansu*-style (traditional handcrafted chest made of fine wood) stairway, sauna walls, and benches—is sided with redwood lumber salvaged from the previous house.

Van Den Berg hired master carpenter Lawrence Wellenstein, a self-trained local barn builder with the reputation as a genius, to help him build the house. Day one on the construction site, Dick rolled back his sleeves to begin building with notes, drawings, and a vision, but no blueprints: "We built it all from scratch. Everything was fitted and built as we were going." As Van Den Berg well understood, no Japanese house would work without the engawa that eases the transition between the interior and exterior. This engawa design was mathematically scaled for a proportioned aesthetic that maintains the Japanese character. The size of the engawa directly relates to the proportions dictated by the roof eave. "The length of the eave

corresponds with the width of the roof. Dropping down from the edge of the roof gives you the width of the engawa," explains Dick.

He took particular care in designing the Japanese elements of the formal entrance. The natural-aged cedar post that flanks the entry and supports the roof gable was a serendipitous find—a salvaged telephone pole "weathered in Wisconsin air." The post is a classic feature of the *tokonoma* (display alcove) in the

Japanese house. The grilled window was a common solution for houses on the crowded narrow streets of old Kyoto. "The home owner could see out, but the screen limited light and screened out passing eyes," says Dick. The entry door was constructed with weathered barn wood.

The design for the interior evolved from the heart, and hearth, outward. Making the copper hood that survived the fire the center of the home, Dick followed the model of the

Japanese folk house, where the *iroya* (open hearth for cooking) is the heart of the home and a source of warmth and family gathering. Positioning the open kitchen at the center of the main living space enabled Lillian, a gourmet cook, to socialize and savor outdoor views of the lake.

The moon gate, perhaps the most romantic feature of the design, was created to bring light into the north interior. Dick directly referenced the window of a teahouse along the

LEFT: Timber-framed terraces of sand, rock, and beach grass step down the dunes to mimic the natural landscape. Boulders were placed to suggest the effect of "nesting" or "resting."

ABOVE RIGHT: This *engawa* (veranda) design was mathematically scaled for a proportioned aesthetic that maintains the Japanese character.

RIGHT: The house nestles in the pine trees.

49

Katsura River in Kyoto that he photographed in the 1970s. The moon gate he designed is crafted with bamboo lattices and illuminated from behind.

To create the scenic gardenscape, Dick removed sixty tons of boulders from a local farmer's stone fences. The stones were individually placed in the sand to give an effect of "nesting or resting" compatible to the house. Timber-framed terraces of sand, rocks, and beach grass step down the dunes to mimic the natural landscape and create a minimal, understated design that becomes part of a total architectural experience. "We took a great deal of care to give the whole house character," says Dick, surveying his project. More than expressing character, the house is rooted to its natural surroundings in true Japanese style.

50

Great repose—serenity, a new tranquility—is the reward for proper

use of each or any material in the true forms of which each is

naturally most capable.

—Frank Lloyd Wright

DIRECTIONS FROM THE NATURAL HOUSE: JAPAN, CHINA, TIBET

THE ORGANIC ARCHITECTURE OF FRANK LLOYD WRIGHT expresses connection with the natural site in ways unprecedented in Western residential architecture by all but the Northwest architects. Wright's ideas, first set out in *The Natural House*, paved the way for experimentation with forms drawn from nature and the use of native materials to relate a building to its environment. Believing that people could be transformed by the experience of living in a house liberated from the traditional box of Western design, Wright favored an open plan in close harmony with the natural world—much as traditional Japanese houses express that relationship. Wright's vision embraced the Japanese reverence for nature and the blend of rusticity and refinement, as well as the striking formal geometry of their distinctive houses.

This chapter looks at three Asian-inspired designs that pay homage to the natural house. John Randal McDonald pushes Wright's famous Honeycomb House in a modernist direction in a house in

THE SOUL OF THE TREE

KROSNICK RESIDENCE

LOCATION: PRINCETON, NEW JERSEY **ARCHITECT:** JOHN RANDAL MCDONALD

Melody Woods III, like our hearts, is so full of memories and the reality of George Nakashima. . . . We see ourselves as the temporary custodians of this home and this collection. Every vista tells us how lucky we are and that we will never forget.

—Arthur and Evelyn Krosnick

ABOVE: Modeled after Wright's organic architecture, McDonald's dignified design for the Krosnick residence conveys the aura of an Asian temple complex.

ABOVE RIGHT: A Japanese garden is created with a river of stones and islands of iris beds.

Secluded in the woods of a peaceful residential neighborhood near Princeton University, the home of Dr. Arthur and Evelyn Krosnick is recognized as an architectural gem in the Frank Lloyd Wright tradition. Architect John Randal McDonald, among the last of Wright's contemporaries committed to a vision of "organic architecture," pushed the vocabulary in an exciting modernist direction. Historically, the first "Melody Woods" McDonald designed for the Krosnicks was built in Bucks County, Pennsylvania. Melody Woods II (built in Princeton in 1979)

was designed expressly for the Krosnicks' collection of furniture by the legendary woodworker George Nakashima, dean of the American Craft Movement. Melody Woods III, rebuilt in 1993 after a fire, houses the replacement furniture created by Nakashima. The home enjoys a unique distinction as the only private residence ever to be furnished entirely in Nakashima's work, from doorknobs and picture frames to exquisitely crafted tables, chairs, benches, and cabinets. With 131 pieces, the Krosnicks acquired one of the largest private collections in the world,

ABOVE LEFT: George Nakashima in the Minguren Studio.

LEFT: Nakashima's Minguren II table and a set of conoid chairs grace the dining room. Evelyn's *omori* (antique Japanese doll) collection is displayed on the shelves of the adjoining library.

FACING: The Arlyn Room honors Nakashima's celebrated "Arlyn Table," his masterpiece in free-form tabletop design. Jonathan Shahn created the bronze sculpture of Nakashima on the cabinet.

next to the Nelson Rockefellers and the Nakashimas.

The famous friendship between George Nakashima and his great patrons, the Krosnicks, dates back to the 1960s, when the couple first visited his studio in New Hope, Pennsylvania. The Krosnicks were mesmerized when they saw George's furniture. As Evelyn describes it, their response to his work was "instantaneous, almost chemical." Over the years the Krosnicks regularly purchased signature pieces, such as the

"conoid" chairs, and commissioned important new work. Their Arlyn table (named for *Ar*-thur and Eve-*lyn*)—an extraordinary eight-foot cross section of redwood burl—is an acknowledged masterpiece in the free-edge tabletop form and perhaps the most dramatic piece Nakashima ever made. (The table presided as symbol of the "tree of life" at a 1990 symposium on the global environmental crisis.)

Melody Woods II gained nationwide celebrity when the home and its Nakashima collection were featured

on the television series *On the Road* in 1987. The Krosnick residence drew special attention, once again, in 1989 when a fire destroyed the house and its priceless furnishings soon after Nakashima's major retrospective, Full Circle, opened at the American Craft Museum in New York. Only the Arlyn table, commissioned for the retrospective, and a double frame with Ben Shahn prints were spared. The Krosnick house was entirely rebuilt under the direction of Tetsu Amagasu, an architect

with the Hillier Group in Princeton. George Nakashima devoted the last year of his life to re-creating much of the lost furniture for his friends and patrons, and passed on the restoration of the Krosnick collection, along with the direction of his studio, to his daughter, Mira Nakashima-Yarnell. In 1993, the house and its furnishings rose "phoenix-like" from the ashes as Melody Woods III (a fate reminiscent of Taliesen, twice destroyed by fire). In its recognition statement, the Historical Society of Princeton said: "Just as Nakashima's life's work reflects the best of both Japanese and American culture, the restored house stands as an amalgam of eastern and western traditions, proving that they can coexist in harmony."

With its deep cantilevered eaves, natural stone pillars, and heavy horizontal lines, the architecture designed by McDonald incorporates classic Wrightean features that complement the free-form contours and cantilevered elements of Nakashima's organic furniture. The architecture also hints at sacred buildings. The multipavilion courtyard design conveys the aura of an Asian temple complex, a theme in harmony with the Buddhist spirit in Nakashima's work (Nakashima was a disciple of Sri Aurobindo in India in the 1930s). The connection with nature emphasized by the architecture accords as well with Nakashima's profound spiritual kinship with the tree, and makes the home a dignified and appropriate setting for the furniture of the great master woodworker.

ABOVE LEFT: The informal dining area in the library features Nakashima's Arlyn I table in claro walnut, and a set of grass-seated chairs.

LEFT: This elegant teacart in the Krosnick dining room features a bitterbrush handle specially selected by Nakashima.

FACING: The Krosnicks welcomed the Princeton community into Melody Woods for lectures and performances in this Music Room.

The architecture itself is a jewel in craftsmanship. The pavilions of the tripartite structure are faceted in hexagon forms, after Wright's famous "Honeycomb House" (his first experiment in non-orthogonal form), with an open plan of interlocking hexagons in natural wood and native stone. The hexagon scheme is carried throughout: it defines the three main pods, vaulted ceilings, skylights, stone fireplace, terrace, and pool design, lending a sacred geometry of proportion to the home. Beveled western red cedar siding clads interior walls and ceilings to complement the warmth and vitality of Nakashima's furniture. As Derek Ostergard (curator of the Nakashima retrospective) points out: "The neutral grain of the cedar used for the walls provides a foil for the vividly grained Persian and claro walnut, rosewood, and Oregon myrtle, which Nakashima employed in the assembly and fabrication of the new furnishings."

As design coordinator for Melody Woods II and III (and founder of Arlyn Design), Evelyn Krosnick recognized that with few fixed walls, furniture placement and lighting would be key to choreographing spatial flow. Interior volumes are defined by intuitive compositions of Nakashima's distinctive furniture, with built-in benches and hanging wall shelves subtly defining transitional passages. Japanese-style screens used throughout provide varying degrees of privacy and bring the soothing effects of filtered light into the house.

Evelyn observes that to live in a home surrounded with Nakashima

furniture is like "living in sculpture." Melody Woods was built to honor Nakashima and his work, and to provide a virtual exhibition gallery. Yet the house was designed to function as a livable environment, not as a museum or sacred space. Ostergard says of the Krosnick home: "It never feels like a shrine because the house and furniture open you up to the outside." For all its mystique, Nakashima's furniture is earthy and functional. Nakashima crafted it to be "kevinized" (coined for his son

Kevin) and enjoyed the distinctive marks created on furniture through its usage. The Krosnicks themselves encouraged that "abuse" by opening their home to the Princeton community for lectures and musical performances in the Music Room. Arthur Krosnick is an esteemed diabetes specialist; Evelyn, a music educator, founded the Greater Princeton Youth Orchestra and served as director.

When the Krosnicks made plans to leave Princeton and Melody Woods III for the next chapter of their lives

in Scottsdale, Arizona, they resolved to give a major portion of their Nakashima furniture new life by auctioning it to the public. New Life for the Noble Tree, the event at Sotheby's in 2006, featured eighty pieces from the Krosnick collection of masterworks by Nakashima, and celebrated an artist and patron collaboration unprecedented in its history. Evelyn says of the event: "Now, more and more lives will be enchanted and enriched by George's furniture, just as our lives have been."

FORM, FUNCTION, TAO

STRAUSS-WILSON RESIDENCE

LOCATION: TELLURIDE, COLORADO **ARCHITECT:** TOMMY HEIN

We pierce doors and windows in making a house, and it is in these spaces, where there is nothing, that the usefulness of the house depends.

—Lao Tzu

ABOVE: The wide curving driveway brings *qi* (subtle energy) into the generous motor court. "The steps were rounded as well to embrace the qi entering the house," explains Hein.

ABOVE RIGHT: The stonework of the residence evokes the texture of the Anasazi ruins at nearby Chaco Canyon.

Asked to describe the philosophy that informs his architecture, Telluride architect Tommy Hein points to the *Tao* ("The Way"): "The *Tao Te Ching* is very integral to my perception. Anything I design has that philosophical foundation." This ancient philosophy of the essential duality and constant flux of nature translates into a dynamic approach to design. Hein never begins a new project with a preconceived idea of what the house might look like but leaves it open to "the people, land, and processes." This openness in the design process allows it to evolve with a fusion

of influences, enabling Hein to explore diverse possibilities that relate and meld a structure to its site and context—climate, topography, history, regional vernacular— vis-à-vis the clients' particular needs and sensibilities.

Steve Strauss and Lise Wilson asked Hein to design a vacation lodge for their family on a wooded site with spectacular views of distant mountain ranges. Hein listened to his clients' desire for "natural balance" and "calmness" and looked to architectural traditions profoundly connected with the natural world: ancient

Pueblo ruins, National Park lodges, Frank Lloyd Wright's "natural houses," and the mountain shrines of ancient Japan. This fusion of related traditions gives the house a monumental character in keeping with the rugged grandeur of the surrounding mountains while creating a fluid statement that morphs between the idioms of a relativized architectural language.

The design embraces the duality of the primary modes of construction. The stone and concrete "earthwork," as Hein describes it, allows the building "to grow from the natural landscape, while its steel-and-timber framing extend aerially to support the sheltering slate roof." Paying homage to the nearby monuments of the Southwest, the stonework evokes the texture of Chaco Canyon ruins. The rustic National Parks vocabulary also enters the home through the post-and-beam construction, broad overhangs, natural timber pergola, and inflected single-gable roof. The timber-frame elements of National Park style share an affinity with the architectural features of seventh-century Japanese shrines (the protruding rafters of the roof are a quotation from the Ise Shrine, the oldest timber-frame structure in the world) and strongly recall the organic architecture of Frank Lloyd Wright.

In his site analysis, Hein conducts a preliminary feng shui study to understand the healthy flow of energy, or qi (pronounced "chee"), in a home's design. Hein works with the Form School principles of feng shui, which depend on intuitive insight, and

FACING FAR LEFT: The paired log timbers that flank the entrance are functional and symbolic. The structural supports recall the Japanese *torii* gate placed in front of temples and shrines to direct *kami* (spirits of nature).

LEFT: Screen-like mahogany windows evoke the simple geometric patterns of *shoji*.

RIGHT: The soapstone fountain and lap pool encourage prosperity from the *yin* properties associated with water, and balance the *yang* energy of the mountains.

emphasize the contours of the landscape to determine the orientation of the house most favorable to encouraging qi. As Hein explains: "The wide, curved driveway brings qi into the generous motor court. The steps are rounded to draw qi into the house. Protection is naturally formed as the site rises to the southwest." To reinforce the home's position, trees were planted and a berm was added to the south in the shape of a dragon. An elegant soapstone fountain and lap pool is positioned in front to encour-

age prosperity from the *yin* properties associated with water, and to balance the *yang* energy of the mountains.

While feng shui figures significantly in the structure's orientation, Japanese elements are more important to its design details. From windows and doors to custom built-in cabinets, Hein took traditional Japanese forms and "distilled them down to a modern essence." The resulting clean modernism was the synthesis of the clients' Asian and contemporary sensibilities. The

screen-like mahogany windows evoke the simple geometric patterns of *shoji*. The steel framework that supports the exterior pergola recalls the Japanese *engawa* (veranda), and the paired timbers near the entrance conjure a *torii* gate (traditionally placed at the entrance of a shrine to mark the boundary between the outside world and the sacred precincts). Hein's strategies for opening the house to nature by "breaking down barriers from interior to exterior" are key to the design. The rooms

63

LEFT: The spruce log timbers frame an expansive view of the mountains and create the feeling of an open-air pavilion.

FACING RIGHT: The corner windows erode the walls, opening the interior to the beauty of nature outside.

FACING FAR RIGHT: Hein based the mahogany doors and *tatami* (mat-covered) platform of the meditation room on historic detailing from traditional Japanese architecture.

relate to the outside with expansive views through window walls, corner windows that erode the enclosure, and square windows that frame small scenes. The main balcony cantilevers over the lower terrace, extending the interior to the outside.

The consistent use of complementary materials throughout the house contributes to a sense of calm. Locally quarried stone is used for exterior walls and terraces as well as for interior wall planes. All of the timbers are recycled Douglas fir and sustainably

harvested spruce. (In its materials and economical vertically stacked massing, the house aspires to an ethics of sustainability important in a mountain region sensitive to the impact of development.) The calm achieved by the materials and details is carried further by the fundamental consistency of proportion, all of which relates to the *ken*, a Japanese system of measurement (about 3 x 6 feet) based on the tatami mat, sized for a reclining body. Hein explains, "This geometry is carried rigorously throughout the whole project.

It is the consistency of proportion that creates a sense of calm." The 1-to-2 ratio in proportions is carried through every element from large to small: the rafters are 6 x 12 inches; the window panes are 2 x 4 feet.

Tectonic consistency demonstrates as well Hein's "deep respect for modernism," where economy and essential treatment of materials accord with the Japanese aesthetic. The revealed joinery of the steel framework highlights the functional beauty of that material much as Japanese joinery

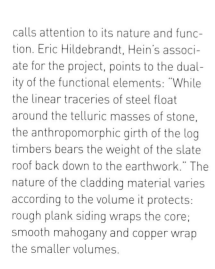

calls attention to its nature and function. Eric Hildebrandt, Hein's associate for the project, points to the duality of the functional elements: "While the linear traceries of steel float around the telluric masses of stone, the anthropomorphic girth of the log timbers bears the weight of the slate roof back down to the earthwork." The nature of the cladding material varies according to the volume it protects: rough plank siding wraps the core; smooth mahogany and copper wrap the smaller volumes.

Duality also characterizes the home's interior space: openness and enclosure, light and dark, public and private space. The first level flows into a "cavern-like" labyrinth of rooms—wine cellar, bedrooms, playroom, exercise room, and meditation room—defined by portals and creating spaces that invite exploration while also providing a sense of shelter and privacy. The second level, by contrast, opens dramatically onto a vaulted "tent-like" communal space that recalls an open-air pavilion with

a massive stone fireplace and views of distant mountains. The great room flows seamlessly into dining and kitchen areas, with the lofty master suite on the third level.

The dialogue between contrasting forms and materials and the flux of opposites—volume and space, symmetry and asymmetry, rustic and refined—create a balanced composition of opposing qualities and forces on every level. That results in a dynamic architectural experience at once timeless and contemporary.

FLOWING TIME, FALLING WATER: A TIBETAN FANTASY

LATHAM RESIDENCE

LOCATION: OAHU, HAWAII   **ARCHITECT:** JOSEPH LANCOR, LANCOR ARCHITECTS, INC.

FACING: The stunning features of the property inspired Lancor to create a home with a "Tibetan monastery" theme.

ABOVE: The central courtyard of the residence features an artificial rockscape with a koi pond and waterfalls fed by a stream. Stepping-stones lead to a hidden Jacuzzi.

Sited on a rugged promontory known as Black Point, once called *Kupiki'o* by the native Hawaiians, which means "raging sea," this romantic residence in Oahu was designed for Larry and Marilee Latham by Joe Lancor, of Lancor Architects, and pays tribute to Hawaii's extraordinary beauty and mystique. Prominent as an architect of luxury resort hotels, apartment buildings, and restaurants, Lancor has also designed significant luxury homes. The architecture of the Latham residence is unusual in the company's portfolio of designs.

For this project, Lancor took a dreamlike approach to the design. The stunning features of the property—with Diamond Head to the west and the vast Pacific Ocean to the south—inspired Lancor to take artistic license with the region's natural and cultural history and create a fantasy—a home with a "Tibetan monastery" theme that appears to have been built centuries before the modern resort-style houses crowding Oahu's shore.

Traditionally, Buddhist monasteries were built on "power spots" like this one, beside dramatic waterfalls or high

LEFT: Lancor designed the tiled roofs, ornamental columns, and courtyard plan to evoke Tibetan monastery architecture.

RIGHT: This guest bedroom situated on the lower level enjoys luxuriant garden and ocean views. The pineapple four-poster bed and carved ceiling fan with a palm-leaf motif add a romantic touch of old Hawaiian character.

in mountain terrain. Frank Lloyd Wright's Fallingwater (Mill Run, Pennsylvania), sited spectacularly on a ledge over a waterfall, also inspired the Latham house design. The Hawaiian location of the property gave Lancor an opportunity to fully express the central principle of Wright's organic architecture: to connect the outside environment with the interior of the home. As Lancor points out, Wright's masterpiece Fallingwater would be

a "happier experience" in Hawaii, where there is far less need for division between the inside living area and the natural world outside than in Pennsylvania.

References from Wright's most famous "natural house" include the prominent roof elements, cantilevered terraces, and the theme of flow, or "flowing through," that informs the design: flow of water, wind, sloping rooftops; flow of movement through the architectural

space. Lancor developed a two-story pavilion-style plan with a central atrium and water garden open to the sky. Living, dining, family rooms, kitchen, study, and guest rooms are featured on the lower level, with the master suite (bedroom, bath, and home office) on the oceanfront wing of the upper level. The tiled-roof pavilion structures, ornamental columns, and courtyard of the residence were designed to evoke Tibetan monastery architecture. These

Asian elements impart the feeling of antiquity and reverence for nature associated with sacred space.

To connect the architecture with the natural terrain, Lancor orchestrated a series of artful illusions. The 1,000-square-foot central courtyard of the residence features an artificial landscape, or "rockscape," with a koi pond and waterfalls fed by a flowing stream. The main waterfall at the upper end of the courtyard flows into a pond (with stepping-stones to a hidden Jacuzzi) around which the home was constructed. The stream flows underneath the living room and cascades into another rock waterfall outside the breezeway. Lancor wanted to make it appear that this simulated water garden existed on the site as a feature of the natural terrain before the construction of the house. To further this effect, sections of supporting column were carved out at the base to fit around "existing" stone.

The architecture is given an aura of antiquity with elements reminiscent of a Tibetan monastery, from tiled roof to pillared walkway, and by simulating the passage of time. Lancor wanted to create the impression that the architecture was built long ago and gradually expanded over the years, and gave the house an "old wing" and "new wing" feeling, in a "pleasingly imperfect, picturesque way." To achieve this effect, certain walls and roof sections are

69

not seamlessly aligned. The impression of antiquity is furthered by the green patina of the roof tiles, "antique" plaster walls, and ornate faux-terra-cotta columns. Art objects and artifacts from the Pacific Islands acquired by Marilee Latham (an interior designer and importer of Asian antiques), along with custom-designed tropical furniture, light teakwood cabinets and detailing, and travertine tile further enhance the old-world mood of the home.

Lancor collaborated with Honolulu sculptor Paul Harada to design the distinctive columns that contribute to the antique character. The vertical steel beams of the steel-frame structure are encased with molded, precast terra-cotta veneers. The architect and sculptor selected Hawaiian motifs for the bas-relief panel of local flowers—bird of paradise, and heleconia, capped with a lawae leaf pattern. These ornate columns define the

interior space of the architecture, framing walls of the ground floor and wrapping around the inner courtyard upstairs.

Lancor also creates the illusion of grand scale in the design. The nine roof sections seem to define a cluster of separate pavilion structures, when, in fact, these rooftops are interconnected. Indoor-outdoor boundaries dissolve and spatial limits expand within the communal space of the residence, where rooms

visually flow together through the open glass-wall design. From within one room, the courtyard garden and parts of other rooms are framed. Ocean views further expand boundaries, and balmy tropical breezes circulate through the open windows, sliding doors, and roofless courtyard. The result of this flowing openness is that the house seems grand beyond its moderate square footage.

By taking a fantasy approach with the Latham house design, Lancor's architecture expresses continuity with Hawaii's sensual tropical beauty while also conjuring a serene mystical world beyond the limits of place and time.

ABOVE LEFT: The dining area adjacent to the kitchen casually overflows into the family room and terrace. Carved terra-cotta columns defining this interior space lend it an air of antiquity.

ABOVE RIGHT: The master bedroom enjoys a private, unobstructed ocean view. The teak-framed bow window expands its modest footprint, and a balcony cantilevers over the water like the deck of a floating vessel.

BELOW RIGHT: The home office in the master suite is an open airy space with stunning views, sensuous hardwood flooring, and art objects and artifacts from the Pacific Islands combined with custom-designed tropical furniture.

72

We need homes for our spirits as well as our bodies. We need to express the special spirit of place and time in our surroundings . . . and live in joyful harmony with them.

—Tom Bender

THE NATURE
OF PLACE

ENVIRONMENTAL DESIGN BEGINS WITH a deep respect for nature along with recognition of ou
connection with the places where we build our homes. Responding effectively to the land requires
an understanding of context—topography, climate, and region—to develop a design that expresses
meaningful connection. And it takes an experienced practitioner to design a building that resonates
with its environment while also answering the needs and desires of the client.

The houses selected for this chapter have a distinct advantage from the start. Each is built in a
spectacular setting close to the restorative beauty of the natural world. Setting alone, however, does
not guarantee that a house will reflect the beauty of its landscape and impart harmony and well-
being to its inhabitants. For the greatest benefits when designing with nature, the architect must
encourage nature to speak to and through us.

Tom Bender, a feng shui master, brings *qi* (subtle life-force energy) into the design of two

BUILDING WITH QI, THE BREATH OF LIFE

BENDER-DE MOLL RESIDENCE
LOCATION: NEAHKAHNIE, OREGON **ARCHITECT:** TOM BENDER

ABOVE: This simple cedar-shingled cottage was designed and built by Bender in 1976. Bender and de Moll are still happy to call it home.

ABOVE RIGHT: An electrical cable spool serves as the table in the Japanese-style dining area, an elevated platform with floor seating.

Tom Bender, a visionary thinker at the forefront of the sustainability movement, has helped to revolutionize Western building practices with his path-breaking research, writing, and "energetic environmental design." In his commitment to ecological architecture, Bender follows in the tradition of the Northwest architects, noted for their deep respect for nature. As a feng shui expert who pioneered the use of this ancient science in America, Bender embraces a more profound connection with nature in his design practice. "Energetic environmental design draws upon considerably broader,

deeper, synthesizing process tools, as opposed to the intellectual-analytical process of conventional design," says Bender. That process involves an intuitive assessment of the optimal flow of subtle energy—or *qi*—of a structure in relation to its environment.

Every feng shui master develops his or her own interpretation of the traditional texts and has a favorite collection of tools, and every situation presents a new design problem or "puzzle" that can be solved in numerous ways. This specialized intuitive art hardly subscribes to the one-size-fits-all strategy of much Western home building. Bender

FAR LEFT: Bender modeled the built-in storage cabinet/staircase after the traditional Japanese *tansu*.

LEFT: Bender selected a door handle with great regional character: "The root's shape keeps alive its difficult life, growing squeezed between the pebbles on the beach."

FACING: The glass walls of the living room slide open for a powerful connection with the ocean environment.

arrives at a site equipped with traditional compass and dowsing rod, but he always listens to the body's wisdom, or gut instinct, to inform him how to direct his intention toward the most energetically beneficial orientation and plan.

Place is key to Bender's design practice, whether designing a residential structure, a church, or a bank. Finding a location already rich in qi is a big head start. With this strategy, he follows the example of the ancient cultures of India, China, and Japan, whose temples and shrines were built on "power spots"—natural sites where spiritual energy flows in abundance. Positive energy, however, can be manifested on any site where it is needed. Bender believes that in the Western world we have lost our vital connection with the environment by creating architecture out of tune with the deeper reality of a place. He promotes the use of native materials to impart meaning and connection, along with recycled materials.

Hiking along the Oregon shore below Neahkahnie Mountain in the 1970s, Tom Bender and Lane de Moll discovered the land that was destined to become their home. Their attraction to the location was so powerful, "it was like the finishing piece of a jigsaw puzzle," says Bender. Neahkahnie, a Tillamook tribal name for "home of the gods," seems a fitting residence for an architect of the sacred who seeks every opportunity to "tap into and activate" qi. The modest home Bender designed and built in 1977, a 1,200-square-foot, cedar-shingled cottage (virtually unchanged

in thirty years) models his design philosophy and sustainable ethics.

The cottage architecture connects with its spectacular natural setting through the use of simple local materials and openness to the outdoors, aesthetic principles important to the Northwest school as well as to the Japanese architectural tradition. The strong Japanese influence in Bender's work is indebted to a Rockefeller fellowship in Japan in the 1960s under the tutelage of Teiji Itoh, architectural historian and author of *Japanese*

Environmental Design. A Japanese aesthetic defines the home's simple, functional interior, economic use of space, and minimalist furnishings.

Bender and de Moll make ingenious use of recycled materials in the décor. Interior walls and cabinets are made of wood recycled from demolished chicken coops.

The house models energy efficiency as well as spatial and material economy with passive solar orientation, and a woodstove (made from a recycled automobile engine block) that serves

as the main heating source. Handmade *shoji* (paper screens) on the stairs bring light into the entry and retain heat in the lower level. In place of a refrigerator, Bender designed a "cool box" tucked away in a kitchen cupboard that draws in cool night air through a series of ventilated compartments.

Thirty years of ocean weather have mellowed the woods in the Bender house, and thirty years living apart from the "deceitful noise of media-dominated city life" have deepened Bender's connection with nature in design.

THERE'S SOMETHING MAGICAL ABOUT THIS PLACE . . .

WILSON RESIDENCE
LOCATION: NEAHKAHNIE, OREGON **ARCHITECT:** TOM BENDER

ABOVE: The low-key décor of the living room contributes to the pervasive calmness of the home.

ABOVE RIGHT: The water garden sets the initial mood of tranquility for the home.

As a peaceful retreat from their busy lives in Portland, Oregon, Dr. Reed and Christina Wilson purchased an ocean-front home with stunning views of the Pacific Ocean on the side of Neahkahnie Mountain. Perfect as it sounds, the Wilsons were uncomfortable in the home. "The footprint didn't feel right," explains Tina. Aware of neighbor Tom Bender's special expertise in handling design problems, the Wilsons requested a consultation. The Reeds were delighted when Bender agreed to take on their home renovation project. "Tom doesn't

just build houses," says Tina. "He's very selective and looks for opportunities to build a unique house in a sacred place." In fact, Tom Bender's statement on his Web site encourages prospective clients whose project does *not* have "unusual possibilities" to look elsewhere.

After a careful analysis of the Wilson home, Tom reported the bad news: the structure was deteriorated to the extent that, sadly, demolition was more cost-effective than needed renovation. The good news was the opportunity to take more powerful advantage of the site to connect

LEFT: The basalt rocks at the gate are the same kind of rock found in the crashing surf below the house.

FACING ABOVE: A madrone driftwood log from the San Juan Islands supports the skylight at the home's entrance.

FACING BELOW: *Prayer flags* is a sculpture by Reed Wilson.

FACING FAR RIGHT: Natural materials vitally connect the home with its environment.

with the mountain, the ocean, and the rhythms of nature. It would seem that a house located in such a beautiful natural setting would provide its owners infinite well-being. However, as Bender points out, "Having a beautiful site to start with does not guarantee positive benefits." In this case the original house didn't work well functionally or beneficially to connect with the spectacular energy of the site.

Once the house was deconstructed and recycled (cedar siding

and cabinets were donated to the Fire Mountain School), and only the leveled lot remained, the Wilsons "fell in love" with the property. Reed Wilson describes the dramatic location: "It's a steep property, a sixty-degree angle up the mountain and 250 feet down toward the ocean, with Oswald West State Park to the north, and ocean to the west and south." For the redesign of their home, the Wilsons envisioned a one-story house "laid on the property," in contrast to the original two-story footprint.

The simple L-shaped cedar-shingled structure Bender designed for his clients settles comfortably and securely into the natural setting. "It's amazing how the house fits perfectly on the lot," says Tina. To create a stronger connection to the waves crashing on the rocks below, Bender relocated the front deck they had anticipated in the design. "The most powerful view is downward to the rocks, and a deck would have blocked connection with that energy," explains Bender. The home enjoys

unobstructed ocean views through seventeen windows, ten of which are floor-to-ceiling height. So much visual exposure and open structure in a different plan might create a sense of vulnerability. However, Tina claims that even with hundred-mile-an-hour winds, the house has a "very safe feeling." Bender explains the paradox: "Designing for views is design based on 'aesthetics,' a surface-based approach resulting from a materialistic culture. A deeper approach, based on mean-

ing and connection to energy, gives a deep reconnection with the rest of creation, and nurtures us with the energetic linkages."

More than a snug sanctuary with enchanting views, the retirement home Bender designed for the Wilsons is "total magic," according to Reed Wilson. "As a neurologist, I don't believe too much in the non-scientific," explains Reed from his Portland home. "But there's something magical about this house, something immeasurable about it."

That "something" would appear to be *qi* energy at work in a marvelous, health-enhancing way. "Everyone is in awe who visits this house," Reed continues. "It's not palatial, it's a nice house in a nice location—part of the magic, of course, is in the location, but it's more than that. I can't put my finger on it. I've been there hundreds of times . . . never had a bad time, never a bad memory. . . . Tom is a magician." A near-death survivor who visited the Wilson home confirmed that mystical aura Reed describes.

"She could see the energy," says Bender. "It made her cry."

Asked to explain how he brings the magic of feng shui into his design practice, Bender comments, "There are many levels of working with energy. Clarity and strength of intention are primary. Work with your intuitive qi-based consciousness, not just your rational mind. Work with an open heart, with a sense of awe toward the complexly simple beauty that creation has manifested in each particular place." Above all, Bender advises to be "in tune with the particular interweavings of life on the site."

Bender finds the intense natural power at the Wilson property and surrounding Neahkahnie area (where his own home is also located) over-powering at times. With thirty-foot waves continually beating on the rock cliffs of the mountain during a storm, whole houses vibrate, and the mountain "resonates like a bell." To ground the Wilson home in the midst of this almost supernatural power, Bender carefully oriented the structure: "The quiet peaceful garden side with yin energy gives relief and balance to the male [yang] energy of the ocean to the west and south."

Natural materials vitally connect the home with its environment. Rock from the region is used for the fireplace, entrance gate, and retaining walls in the garden. The basalt rocks at the gate are the kind of rocks

LEFT: The dining room flows from the main living space and expands to an open deck for outdoor entertainment.

RIGHT: The light emanating from the richly resonant woods of this corridor seems almost palpable.

one finds in the crashing surf below the house. The reverence for simple natural materials that Bender shares with the Japanese is expressed in his consistent use of untreated native cedar for the exterior. The center post that supports the skylight at the entrance is a madrone driftwood log from the San Juan Islands salvaged from the Neahkahnie beach. *Shoji*-themed doors and windows bring the soothing effects of natural light into the interior.

Asked whether he had any other tricks up his sleeve, Bender says, "Pay careful attention to *every* problem you have to solve in the design, and find a solution that effortlessly fills all the needs, not just the primary one." The Wilson house is a prime example. After the initial house plan was drawn up, the Wilsons decided they wanted to add a studio above the garage. To meet height restrictions, Bender's design solution was to lower the level of the entire

house. By dropping the living room floor two feet, the study and the dining room gained ocean views across the living room. Sitting steps were created along two sides. Lowering the house level required the construction of a stone retaining wall. That wall inspired the creation of the Japanese water garden at the home's entrance that now seems inevitable to the design. This garden sets the peaceful tone for the experience as you enter the gate of the Wilson home.

ZONED FOR THE TROPICS: "THIRTY-SECOND VISIONS" FROM THE SOURCE

PRIVATE RESIDENCE

LOCATION: OAHU, HAWAII **ARCHITECT:** CAREY SMOOT, SOURCE TROPICAL

ABOVE: The beauty of organic architecture is expressed with lava stone, ironwood shingles, and fluid natural lines. This native tropical design perfectly harmonizes with the exquisite Hawaiian setting.

The Confucian saying "If you enjoy what you do, you'll never work another day in your life" seems to be the wisdom scripted for Carey Smoot, architectural designer and founder of Source Tropical, a company specializing in authentic tropical architecture and design products (Hawaii and Bali). Describing some of the highlights of his "adventures in architecture," Smoot pauses to remark: "I've never worked a day in my life and I've never had a vacation." The boundary between work and play is a fluid one for this maverick designer whose field research for the development of his

tropical portfolio began in the Philippines (Smoot taught jungle survival during the Vietnam War) and has extended throughout Pacific Asia. "I went to every one of the twenty-seven provinces of Indonesia and the Philippines to study tropical indigenous designs, as primitive people like to articulate their culture as well," says Smoot. In his travels off the beaten path, Smoot studied the practical applications of natural materials as well as native cultural beliefs to understand "connection with place."

On the leading edge of the environmental design movement in the 1970s,

Smoot founded Envirotecture, a company that pioneered the use of elliptical domes and nonrectilinear structures based on forms in nature. In 1974, Smoot designed the Krishnamurti School in Ojai, California. J. Krishnamurti had some daunting requests for the architecture. "It had to be a form of architecture never done in America; constructed of wood; built to last 100 years," recalls Smoot. And most intriguing, "When you enter, you lose your sense of self." Presented with a design challenge, Smoot typically experiences a "thirty-second vision" from which to develop the plan. His epiphany for the Krishnamurti School resulted in an organic design that creates "the impression of movement"—a modified hexagon plan with no ninety-degree angles and an "ocean wave roof."

By moving beyond the box with his unconventional designs, Smoot attracted Hollywood celebrities and pop icons as clients. Turning his attention to Hawaii in the 1980s (Smoot grew up in Oahu), he put a serious tropical spin on luxury residential architecture.

During his years designing houses in Hawaii, Smoot has exerted an influence "to turn Hawaiian architecture around to tropical designs based on Pacific Asian designs." Smoot caught the first wave of the Hawaiian Renaissance (and the movement to reconstruct Hawaiian identity) and

LEFT: The dining area transforms into an open-air pavilion with sliding doors, and flows seamlessly onto the *lanai* (veranda).

RIGHT: The hand-carved bowls on the mantel are made of koa wood, the most prized cabinet and furniture wood in Hawaii (and currently on the endangered species register).

helped to revive the rich vernacular that had evolved through centuries of Pacific migrations. For luxury residential projects, this meant a more intimate, human-scaled and natural aesthetic in harmony with the spirit of the tropical environment, with native features such as the *lanai* (veranda) and open—*ohana* style—plan with pavilion structures arranged in a traditional "family" grouping. The Hawaiian word *ohana*, which refers to kin group or extended family, and by extension defines a way of life, has become popularized as an architectural style suited to casual island living.

The distinctive natural architecture of this residence in windward Oahu, grounded into a spectacular oceanfront site, features a Carey Smoot interpretation of Old Hawaiian style. The architecture was designed for a couple that travels much of the year, but they wanted to build a primary residence in Hawaii with ample space for friends and family. "Ohana is featured in the main floor plan as the owners entertain a lot and often have extended family members visiting," explains Smoot. The original house on the property was converted into separate guest quarters, becoming part of a multistructural compound that includes a detached bathhouse with Jacuzzi and a garage in addition to the main attraction—a new two-story pavilion.

Smoot never orients architecture parallel to the property but

sites it toward the wind and arc of the sun. In this case, the structures are sheltered from behind by the mountain, and face into the sunrise and the northwestern trade winds that blow most of the time on the windward side of Oahu. The main *hale* (house) features an open plan that integrates kitchen, dining, and living spaces on the lower level and flows onto a wraparound lanai that takes full advantage of the wind. The owners commented that the constant

breezes flowing through the house eliminate the need for insect screens or air-conditioning. The master bedroom and bath on the second level also provide a luxurious open-air experience with a private terrace overlooking the ocean.

Smoot is known for his signature roofs. Asked to explain the inspiration for the distinctive roof featured on all three hales of this compound, Smoot offered to "pontificate on tropical indigenous design":

I found myself in the basement of the Bishop Museum in Honolulu looking at Captain Cook's first voyage into the harbor. As this was in the days before cameras, Cook had a man that drew illustrations of the Hawaiian structures called hales. They had a certain roof pitch that was different from the roof styles of the Tahitians, Samoans, and Marquesas who first populated the Hawaiian Islands. I later found out in my projects all through the South Pacific and Micronesia that

FACING: The outer walls of the master bedroom slide open to the deck for breezy open-air living. Sleek modern fixtures and cabinets combine with natural textures and old colonial touches—a freestanding bathtub and carved koa rocker.

RIGHT: The open ceiling, fashioned in tropical hardwoods and bamboo, gives the master bedroom a strong native character. The pineapple four-poster bed, crafted in koa wood, and the antique wardrobe reflect the Victorian style of Hawaii's colonial days.

each culture produced little architectural nuances so as not to look like the neighboring boys. There were certain elements such as roofs and carvings that stood them apart.

The roof concept for the three hales of the Oahu residence draws from traditional elements of Hawaii's mixed Pacific Island architectural lineage: fish-scale ironwood shingles with a modified rolled hip-and-gable design. Smoot points out, "The roofs were much higher in old Hawaii. Building codes today don't allow roofs of great height. So what you see in the main hale is a compromise. The roof pitch is 8:12, hip and gable." The height of the thatch roof on the bath hale would not be allowed in today's building code of Honolulu County. Smoot explains that the skirt roof extending horizontally from the main roof is an element that you see all over the tropical world. "It shades the lower walls and windows during midday heat. The roof works well in the rain as well." It also has aesthetic value by breaking the tall single wall surface halfway.

Smoot's tropical design vocabulary for this project represents a colorful fusion of styles and materials. "This residence in Windward Oahu includes coconut posts, carved merbau for the center column, Iliili lavastone platforms, and thatch roofs of ironwood and grass," explains Smoot. All of these elements, except

for the lava-stone platforms, were used in various ways in previous residential designs. Although the concept and much of the material for this project are Hawaiian in origin (the koa wood cabinets are from the big island of Hawaii, the lava stone is from Oahu), Smoot imported tropical materials from Indonesia, Queensland, and the South Pacific: shingles from Borneo, grass from Balik, merbau from Irian Jaya with carving from Bali, boxbrush flooring

from Queensland, and coconut posts from North Sulawesi.

This unpretentious tropical architecture, settled comfortably beside the neighboring mountains and ocean, seems quite at home on this Hawaiian island. The authentic "native" feel to the design is indebted to Smoot's intuitive approach to creating architecture that harmonizes with its environment.

ABOVE: The rolled hip-and-gable roof with iron-wood shingles is a Smoot signature roof developed from research of native tropical vernacular and years of experimentation.

FACING: The bath *hale* (house), featuring a private Jacuzzi, is decorated with imported Italian tile and a hand-stenciled Hawaiian motif. The roof is made of thatched grass.

RAINFOREST LIGHT

SLEEPING PAVILION

LOCATION: MOUNT RAINIER, WASHINGTON **ARCHITECT:** PHILIP BECK, BECK STUDIO

ABOVE: The pavilion's "transparent skin" takes advantage of the filtered light of the forest to become a light-filled vessel.

ABOVE RIGHT: The screen-like wall framing and skylight roof structure are enclosed with translucent lightweight polycarbonate sheets.

Set like a lantern in a misty primeval forest, this enchanting sleeping pavilion designed by architect Philip Beck was inspired by his childhood adventures in the magical rainforest of Mount Rainier, where the Beck family owned a 1920s log cabin. The detached modern pavilion structure is perched on a site above the old log cabin, and provides additional sleeping space for guests. This inspired project captures the spirit of Beck's architectural design philosophy, which emphasizes place (climate, culture, and topography), sensitivity to the environment, and exploration of

new technologies responsive to his clients' needs and their surroundings—principles that follow directly in the tradition of the Northwest architects.

The design concept and the site for the pavilion "came out of the quality of light in the forest," explains Beck. The light changes dramatically on the property according to the density of the forest. Beneath its dark canopy of trees, the old cabin receives little sunlight. The new structure takes advantage of an area with light penetrating through a less dense, semi-open part of the forest featuring

alder trees instead of the dark cedar growing around the cabin. "The light filtering through the tree canopy presented an opportunity for transparency in structure and use of subtle light," says Beck. When set against the new structure, located in an open area of ferny undergrowth and vine maples, the old log cabin shaded by huge cedar trees virtually creates a yin-yang energy pair.

The steep forest terrain and lack of road access to the site presented a distinct building challenge. For Beck,

however, accustomed to trekking in mountain regions from Colorado to the Himalayas (Beck designed Tiger Mountain Pokhara Village, an award-winning eco-resort in Nepal), the site's location was not a deterrent to construction. Beck and his design collaborators, architects Frank Dill and Cordell Steinmetz—Beck's former classmates at Harvard University Graduate School of Design—carried the building materials by hand up the steep footpath to the site. The project took them four months to complete.

The upper layer of the soil, composed of volcanic ash, inspired an innovative and noninvasive design solution. As Beck explains: "The soft volcanic soil made it easy for us to dig holes for the concrete piers that support the wood posts. We elevated the structure to minimize disturbance of the site—it touches the ground at only a few points." The effect is that the structure "hovers over the forest floor." Beck made use of natural woods for the framework of the pavilion to blend it with the

natural setting. The freestanding cedar posts supporting the structure were harvested on-site.

Interior walls and ceilings were constructed in pine. The screen-like wall framing and skylight roof structure are enclosed with translucent lightweight 4 x 12 polycarbonate sheets. This "transparent skin" allows the building to take advantage of the filtered light of the forest to become "a light-filled vessel." The structural framework of the pavilion design appears so thin it virtually dissolves into the forest. By day, in certain light, the pavilion mirrors the surrounding trees and disappears into them. At night, the pavilion transforms into a glowing lantern reminiscent of a Japanese *andon* (paper-screened lantern).

Although Beck makes no overt references to the Japanese architectural tradition in the pavilion project, he incorporates the aesthetic in "an abstract way"—foremost, "in the attitude toward site and the respect for natural setting." (Beck brings to his work a Harvard degree in East Asian studies as well.) The structure's simple formal geometry and the lightness and transparency of its materials are indebted to Japanese design principles. "The light infill between the posts of the structure resemble the lightness of Japanese wood architecture," says Beck—in particular, the effects created by *shoji* (grid-patterned Japanese screens). The Japanese art of illumination encourages the architecture to express subtleties of light and

LEFT: By day, in certain light, the pavilion mirrors the surrounding trees and disappears into them.

RIGHT: The light, translucent infill of the structure creates a tent-like intimacy with the forest.

98

shadow, and dissolves the boundaries between indoors and outdoors for a rich appreciation of nature, a naturalistic aesthetic explored with modern materials in Beck's light vessel.

Contrasting the forms and materials of the sleeping pavilion with those of the old cabin, Beck creates a fascinating visual counterpoint. The old log cabin, crafted of whole timbers, expresses a kinship with the trees, an intimate connection that extends from rustic exterior to cozy interior walls.

The pavilion's sleek lines and high-tech reflective materials express a connection with the forest in a different, more metaphysical way through the immaterial (spiritual) qualities of light that play on its surface. The phantom trees reflected on its surface skin are visible from within, creating a seamless connection with the outdoors and the mystical beauty of the natural world.

LITTLE HOUSE ON THE BIG ISLAND

OHANA HOUSE

LOCATION: NIULII, KOHALA, HAWAII **ARCHITECT:** CUTLER ANDERSON ARCHITECTS

Ohana House is built on seventy-five grassy acres overlooking the Pacific Ocean. On the windward side of the big island of Hawaii, nature's presence is powerful.

Prominent for architecture rooted in the Pacific Northwest tradition, Cutler Anderson Architects of Bainbridge Island, Washington, has designed many award-winning public buildings, memorials, and private residences. The firm's diverse portfolio expresses a common theme: attention to how the architecture reflects the "nature and significance of the place" and the "nature and power of materials." For Jim Cutler, who has experienced different landscapes all over the world, stepping onto the site of a prospective project is "like walking into a classroom

full of children all raising their hands and shouting, 'Call on me!'" With each new project, the architect must respond to a "roomful of shouting things"—land, institutions, topography—to integrate a building's forms and materials with its context. "To get the cacophony of voices in harmony, to get everything to tell its story in relation to its neighbors is very difficult," says Cutler. Yet Cutler and his partner, Bruce Anderson, have mastered the art of making the complex language of architecture look simple—almost inevitable—in their designs.

This contemporary residence in Kohala, Hawaii, located on a blustery hilltop on the windward side of the big island, invited nature to play a big role in its design. The owners, who live in the San Francisco Bay Area, purchased the seventy-five-acre property, the former site of a sugar mill, to build a family compound. The wife (whose parents are Chinese) was born and raised on Oahu, and the owners frequently return to Hawaii with their children to visit relatives. Ohana ("guest") House is the first of

a three-structure compound planned for the property. The clients wanted to experiment by building their guesthouse on the highest part of the site to capture the most dramatic ocean views.

The small scale of the 2,600-square-foot house relative to the vast Pacific Ocean draws attention to its essential role as shelter. Its low-profile functional design was driven by the circumstances of weather patterns on the big island's north-east coast. The shape, structure, and

position of the plan elements were "framed to protect the owners from the constant ten- to forty-knot-per-hour trade winds while still providing views of the ocean and wind-free access to warm sunlight." The simple U-shaped plan comprises three wings—kitchen-dining and living area, bedroom wing (master suite and two bedrooms), and a studio and garage wing—that open onto a sheltered courtyard with pool and gardened terrace. The front of the house is oriented to enjoy protected

LEFT: The design of the house shelters the pool terrace from the constant trade winds and opens it to ocean views through expansive glass walls of the house.

RIGHT: Skylights, generous windows, and open rafters bring dramatic light into the residence at all hours.

180-degree ocean views. The courtyard, by contrast, faces into the hillside and the arc of the sun to shelter it from the wind.

For the Ohana House design, materials were selected to adapt the architecture to its unique environmental circumstances while also highlighting their inherent beauty. "You need to examine and understand the nature of each material and use it in a way that allows it to reveal its best qualities . . . the strengths for which it is designed." This modernist approach,

focused on an essential treatment of material, accords with the Japanese aesthetic. Asked about the affinity his architecture shares with that tradition, Cutler remarks, "In traditional Japanese architecture, each material is allowed to completely express itself . . . materials are fully revealed. In our work, we follow a similar line of logic." Cutler describes this correspondence as analogous to "parallel evolution" (the phenomenon in which life forms with similar characteristics evolved centuries and continents

apart as a result of adaptations to similar ecosystems).

In designing a building, the architect must differentiate between materials for greatest effect. "Each element gets to tell a different story," says Cutler. The rugged stonework at Ohana House tells the story of the region's ancient history. On the way to the property, a huge rock pile marks the remains of a sacrificial temple—a reminder that the big island was once Kamehameha country. Dramatically carved canyons

Cut lava stone featured
in the terrace tile
work extends into the
kitchen and corridors
for a seamless indoor-
outdoor transition.
The elegantly simple,
custom-designed cabi-
net serves as a casual
partition between the
kitchen and adjoining
living area.

LEFT: Interior paneling and custom-designed cabinetry featured in the baths and kitchen are fashioned in Hawaiian-grown eucalyptus.

RIGHT: The building is anchored to the rock-based land through steel tie-downs visually laced into the rafters and pinned into the stone foundation.

FACING BELOW: Locally quarried A'A' lava rock is used for the stacked-stone features.

not far down the road and sheer cliffs plunging to the ocean below the property testify to the island's volcanic history. For Cutler, battered lava-stone walls seemed very appropriate for this project. Locally quarried A'A lava rock is used for the stacked stone exterior and interior walls. Cut lava stone is featured in the terrace tile work, extending into the kitchen-dining area adjacent to the courtyard for a seamless indoor-outdoor transition.

Wood with a tropical island lineage is the major element of this finely crafted house. Cedar-shingled exterior siding is a Cutler Anderson trademark. Where applicable, woods indigenous to the islands were used throughout the interior. Floors are tamarind, a species of tropical African hardwood introduced to the Hawaiian Islands in the eighteenth century. Interior paneling and custom-designed cabinetry featured in the kitchen, cabinet/partition, and

baths are fashioned in grown eucalyptus. Str frame elements, inclu and beams, rafters, ar crafted in Douglas fir. rail components of the made of teak.

Exposed structural composition—the visib nents combined with t timber framework and masonry—call attentic tion of these durable n

the need for strong shelter in this environment. The building is anchored to the rock-based land through steel tie-downs "visually laced into the rafters and pinned into the stone foundation." The contemporary roofline that contributes to the architecture's visual impact and snug earth-hugging character was engineered to counter the force of winds. The compound-pitch metal roofs of the three adjoining wings of the residence pitch in two directions: one side of the roof section tips northwest toward the wind, and the other side is pitched to match the angle of the hill on which the house is built, to shelter the courtyard from the elements.

With its human scale and high-performance minimalist design, Ohana House defines the essence of shelter. Less house, more openness to the outdoors, invites nature to coexist with the design. The home's seamless interface and serene, uncluttered décor make way for the bigger events of nature.

108 The integration of Asian design concepts into American house design has strong appeal for those looking for "natural" alternatives to the Western home standards.

HIFTING CONTEXTS: AST/WEST FUSION

THIS CHAPTER TAKES A LOOK at two home renovations that playfully shift traditional Western house designs toward the East. Worlds apart in region and vernacular, a rural New Jersey farmhouse and a Florida ranch house are transformed into hybrid designs with a multicultural Asian edge.

American house design can hardly get more traditional than the clapboard farmhouses of New Jersey. To modify their eighteenth-century farmhouse to suit their Asian and modern sensibilities, artist Bennett Bean and Cathy Bao Bean (first-generation Chinese American daughter) approached the redecorating process with humor. The addition of a modern living room and an gallery makes a bold departure from tradition. The Beans called in the designer Clodagh for final editing advice.

To bring a more natural spirit into the home, sometimes it's not enough to add a little bam

THE DREAM OF THE NOT-TOO-PERFECT HOUSE: A LESSON IN MULTICULTURAL RENOVATION

BEAN RESIDENCE

LOCATION: NEW JERSEY **DESIGNER:** BENNETT BEAN WITH CLODAGH, DESIGN CONSULTANT

ABOVE: The new addition blends seamlessly with the eighteenth-century farmhouse.

ABOVE RIGHT: The iconic American silo is given an Asian-themed roof.

BELOW RIGHT: Whimsy and color enliven many corners of the Bean residence.

Do the parts equal more than the whole? That philosophical question, posed by Cathy Bao Bean in an article on multicultural identity in *The Journal of College & Character* (November 2005) might be instructively applied to the case of Cathy and Bennett Bean's home renovations. Expatriates from the New York art scene of the 1970s, the Beans turned down a Soho loft space to purchase an eighteenth-century New Jersey farmhouse. Add thirty years of experimental renovations and the result would seem inevitable: many changes whose parts are irreducible to any particular design concept. Inevitable, that is, for artist Bennett Bean, known in the art world for his wildly decorative ceramic vessels (found in museum collections from the Whitney to the Smithsonian), and his wife, Cathy, former philosophy professor and master of the Chopsticks-Fork Principle (and author of a book by that title), who encourages people to "locate the playgrounds and minefields of being at least bicultural," with the advice, "If you don't have a sense of humor—*pretend!*"

Bennett Bean undertook most of the renovations for the house and the various

LEFT: The rolling landscape behind the residence features garden statuary designed by Bean, such as a "pocket Parthenon," a classical terra-cotta pergola.

RIGHT: A Barcelona lounge chair in leather and steel (vintage van der Rohe) sits opposite a Colonial American bench.

114

detached buildings on the property's ten acres of rolling farmland, including a barn studio, greenhouse, and garden structures, such as a "pocket Parthenon"—a classical pergola with terra-cotta columns. The latest installments of this ongoing renovation story include the addition of a spacious wing on the original farmhouse and the conversion of an old silo on the property into a retreat with a pagoda-style roof.

The functional and the artistic happily overlap at the Bean residence,

where Bennett's artistic experiments are hardly confined to the studio, but extend to the interior faux painting of walls and woodwork. Bean began experimenting with layering paint to simulate effects long before "faux painting" hit mainstream American décor. Cathy witnesses this eternal home-improvement process with stoic amusement (see *The Chopsticks-Fork Principle*). While she values the functional, Cathy has a natural—or is it a cultural—affinity for the fluid

dimensions of a work of art or a home design not aspiring to be complete or "perfect." From a Chinese perspective, "there is no perfect, for there is always room for improvement in an always-changing world, and 'ideal' is a moving target, a matter of balancing chaos and order through cyclical time frames." An I-Ching philosophy of change informs Bean's artistic practice, "a dance between control and chance" that values process over finished product.

The new addition gave Bean his "first chance to do structure." Bean developed a dual-purpose design that answered their need for a spacious living room to entertain friends as well as an exhibition space for displaying his latest work to clients. The new structure fuses seamlessly with the old farmhouse (following the rural American practice of adding wings with expanding needs). Clapboard siding and eyebrow windows were selected to match the

features of the original building. The conservative design of the façade is carried into the traditional foyer of the residence. Once inside, however, the prominent Asian theme of the home is announced in the décor. The foyer gives way to a modern living-room-cum-art-gallery adjacent to the Beans' traditional dining room.

The Beans called in the designer Clodagh, a friend and business associate, to edit Bennett's ideas for the interior (Bean's sideline company,

Columbine, completed the architectural terra-cotta for Clodagh's first major project). Clodagh advised against too many windows in the design and suggested that Bennett think about creating a niche. Clodagh's design firm completed the layout of the lighting. With the exception of the sculptural Ingo Maurer light, the fixtures are inset to wash light from the walls above the fireplace. Recessed skylights echo the pattern of ribbon windows

above the glass wall of doors to the garden. Bean selected a barrel-vaulted ceiling as an alternative to the standard peaked roof. Its lofty curvature softens the angular thrust of the composition.

Faux-painted walls lend the room an air of mystery and antiquity, an effect that is almost a Clodagh signature. Atmospheric layering of paint creates the illusion of eroded spatial boundaries. Bean developed this technique through years

of experimentation with layered surface not only on the walls of his home but also in the decoration of his ceramic vessels, known for their dematerialization of spatial volume. The result of the Bean-Clodagh collaboration is both evocative and elegantly minimalist.

The new room features a playful mix of decorative elements and furnishings—Modernist, Asian, and American Colonial. The décor complements the spirit of Bean's ceramic art,

an esoteric blend that combines the preciousness of Persian miniatures, the primitivism of Native American pots, and the freedom of abstract painting. The Beans' inspired collision of styles and periods happily combines family heirlooms—period pieces such as a Chippendale cabinet—with flea market finds, eBay purchases, and Asian art collected in the Beans' extensive travels.

In the gallery area of the room, Bean displays the shifting inventory

LEFT: Bean created the innovative "dot painting wall," an adjustable shelving system to exhibit new work.

RIGHT: A contemporary red sponge chair is paired with a Tibetan robe.

of his latest creations, which now include Tibetan-inspired rugs designed by Bennett and woven at a factory in Nepal. Bean designed an innovative "dot painting wall," an adjustable shelving system, to exhibit new sculptural pieces. As for now, he says, "History—older work—is in the kitchen, contemporary, in the new room." The new room, like the rest of the house, is ever changing. After thirty years of continual meta-morphosis in Bennett's redecorating schemes, Cathy is only marginally aware of the changes: "It is always changing, but I hardly notice it." (Cathy only discovered that some furniture was missing from the house when it appeared in a show for Bennett's work.)

The walls of the "final" addition are up, solid and built to last. But the Bean home promises to remain a work in progress. Cathy remarks, "Maybe we'll renovate every twenty years"—not as a nod to feng shui tradition so much as a wink at the Chinese gods who might punish her for the audacity to think of her house as perfect.

A FISH STORY:
FROM THE BALINESE

GREENE RESIDENCE

LOCATION: FLORIDA **ARCHITECT:** JON OLSON, PEACOCK & LEWIS, ARCHITECTS

ABOVE: The cleanly sculpted exterior has an eye-catching design that plays with geometric forms: squares, rectangles, and trapezoids.

ABOVE RIGHT: "We wanted a roof with the feeling of lifting off, reaching up to the sky," says Ana.

With its finny peaks and wings, this joyous architecture on the intercoastal waters of southeast Florida resembles a fantastic hybrid transplanted from a dream—part bird, part fish, part exotic plant. Its inventive and unlikely forms, inspired by Balinese villages and Frank Lloyd Wright houses, give the Greene remodel an earthy yet ultra-refined character. Bob and Ana worked closely with architect Jon Olson, of Peacock & Lewis, Architects, to develop this design for their home.

The existing house on this site, when the Greenes purchased the property in 1994,

was a custom island-ranch design. Bob and Ana envisioned, in its place, a house that would "bring the outside in" to give their family greater connection with the beauty of their surroundings. Bob and Ana wanted the new architecture to be dynamic but aesthetically scaled to fit the property, not overblown. Most of all, they wanted a warm and inviting design with a natural yet contemporary aesthetic that would express continuity with their coastal environment.

The original footprint was transformed into a more fluid, open plan with three interconnected pods: a central communal

LEFT: The sweeping gable of the pool terrace is reminiscent of the simple thatched-roof Balinese lean-to.

RIGHT: The floor of the master bedroom is Brazilian cherry hardwood, selected for its warmth and richness. Ana and Bob chose the hand-carved ladder from Mali, Africa, (called a *dogen*) because it reminded them of a dancing human figure.

space including living room, dining room, kitchen, and den; an adjacent master bedroom wing with design studio and home office; and a wing on the opposite side with children's rooms and a guest suite.

The Greenes played a major role in the redesign. Frank Lloyd Wright's "natural house" philosophy was their point of departure. "Almost the way a tree grows out of the ground, the home should have that connection to the earth," says Ana. As the three-year planning process evolved

in collaboration with Jon Olson, the Greenes were drawn toward the tropical vernacular of Indonesia. "In the approach to feeling, we were pulled by the Indonesian, especially the Balinese, aesthetic and how those homes fit into their natural environment," explains Ana. That naturalness, combined with Wright's experiments with organic shapes to get beyond the box of Western architecture, informs the design.

The cleanly sculpted front exterior has an eye-catching design that

plays with geometric forms—squares, rectangles, trapezoids—and presents a slightly skewed symmetry. The trapezoidal façades below the roof are cleverly mirrored in the shape of the window flanking the door. Its asymmetrical placement creates the impression that it was built around a natural rock formation. The masonry forms throughout the design have that natural character.

The Jacksha residence in Fresno, California, designed by Wright's protégée Arthur Dyson, inspired the

striking roof design. "We wanted a roof with the feeling of lifting off, reaching up to the sky," says Ana. Olson's interpretation of the Dyson design exploited the rooflines of the original structure: "The winglike configuration came from the steep-pitched (12 x 12) profiles from the original house," explains Olson. "The sheathing on the underside with tongue-and-groove wood gave it a Prairie-style feeling."

Olson designed an impressive "flying wedge" design for the entrance

that extends into the ceiling of the foyer. This innovative architecture was inspired by old shipyard design "where the shipbuilders pieced the keel together," explains Olson. "The idea evolved from the need for a ridge beam at that location that could express itself as a structural element. I came up with the idea of a keel to enhance the connection." The flying wedge entry matches the sweeping gable of the waterside lanai. A visual corridor from the foyer through the interior to the pool terrace links the

front and back sides of the house so that, upon entering, the eye is immediately directed outdoors.

The waterfront side of the residence modulates into a more traditional spin on the Balinese: a village compound theme with pitched gable roofs, slate shingles, and deep eaves. The cluster of rooftops in different angles and sizes is reminiscent of the casual evolution of a traditional Balinese village where structures added over time are not perfectly aligned. The renovation

took advantage of the fan-shaped property, which directs its widest part toward the water, to bring light and dramatic views into the home. Glass walls wrap the three pods of the waterfront exterior to enhance that connection.

The emphasis on natural textured forms and materials in their home expresses a wabi-sabi philosophy of life that Ana and Bob share: "The imperfection of life is the perfection of life." The home features an array of exotic woods, from mahogany ceilings to Brazilian cherry floors, along with earth-colored Indian slate and natural stone masonry. The exterior stucco was selected for its "soft, undulating texture." This earthy natural palette balances the clean contemporary lines of the architecture's structural steel elements.

Ana's design studio is perched on an upper gallery accessed by a spiral staircase from the master bedroom. Ana is a Portuguese-born jewelry artist who studied with Bulgari's head designer. For this space, Ana wanted to create a peaceful sanctuary for creative work and relaxation. Simplicity, integrity, "continuity of line" (signature elements of Ana's jewelry), and natural textured materials, such as bamboo for the cathedral ceiling, an inherent element of Balinese style, characterize her studio. For the staircase, Ana and Bob selected an openwork floating steel form. "From the banister, it

FACING FAR LEFT: An intimate yet worldly personal space with Ana's elegant signature in the décor: bamboo cathedral ceiling, Brazilian wood sculpture, and a collection of found objects, such as shells from the islands, in a sculptural niche that serves as "a loose altar and suggests peace."

LEFT: The presence of the ocean is brought symbolically into the home in the dining area, elusively defined by a glass wall designed to resemble eroded sea glass and framed at the base with a curvilinear row of slate tiles.

RIGHT: The whimsical sculptural furniture by American Arts and Crafts master Wendell Castle—the mandolin-shaped coffee table and funky armoire—seems quite at home in this environment. The chair designed by Howard Werner was carved from a cross section of eucalyptus.

feels like you're standing at the railing of an ocean liner," says Ana. To integrate the studio into the primary design concept, Olson repeated the window design and gable form of the main pod.

However light and "Balinese" in spirit, the architecture of the Greene residence is heavily built. The gabled roofs and framework are designed to withstand seasonal bouts of extreme weather. Bob's real estate and development company served

as the building contractor for the project. "The home's structural envelope is constructed of 2 x 6-foot framing, with metal strapping from the roof to the foundation. The windows are special high-impact laminated glass able to withstand up to 140-mile-per-hour winds," explains Bob. As a testament to the strength of the structure, only months after the Greenes' renovation project was completed in 2004, their home weathered its first major hurricane.

Seasonal storms aside, the Greenes find the experience of living close to the ocean peaceful and rejuvenating. With the home's stronger orientation toward the water, they now have the "illusion of being alone on an island." Ana enjoys sitting at the waterfront in the early-morning hours, watching the birds fly from the nearby spoil island. Bob keeps his sport fisherman at the dock ready at a moment's notice.

123

124   Architecture implies a constant rediscovery of dynamic human

qualities translated into form and space.

David Miller and Robert Hull

DESIGNS ON THE BOUNDARIES: NEITHER EAST NOR WEST

WITH THE NEED FOR INTELLIGENT design solutions as we move into the twenty-first century, architects working in the modern tradition take the exploration of new materials and building methods to a degree beyond anything considered by their predecessors. This chapter looks at the cutting-edge designs of four modernists: Maya Lin, Jim Cutler, Craig Curtis, of the Miller/Hull Partnership, and Shigeru Ban. Their vibrant architecture expresses economy of means, primacy of material, dissolution of spatial boundaries, and sensitivity to context. These design emphases overlap the priorities of the Asian, especially the Japanese, aesthetic that has captured the imagination of modern minimalists since the days of Mies van der Rohe.

The chapter features works of wit, innovation, and resourcefulness: an apartment in New York with shape-shifting components designed by Maya Lin; an estate for a vintner in Napa Valley designed by Jim Cutler that speaks the language of the wine country; an island residence in Puget

HOUSE OF MANY CHANGES: A "SMART HOME" FOR CITY LIVING

PRIVATE RESIDENCE

LOCATION: NEW YORK **ARCHITECT:** MAYA LIN, MAYA LIN STUDIO

ABOVE: "I envisioned a home that could fold in on itself, like origami or a transformer toy, changing its shape or function depending upon how it was used," says Lin.

ABOVE RIGHT: The stairs unfold, origami-like, in two directions.

Architect, artist, environmental designer, Maya Lin works on the boundaries "somewhere between science and art, art and architecture, public and private, east and west," as she describes her fluid position (*Boundaries*). Best known for her elegant architecture for public spaces—large-scale abstract monuments, notably the Vietnam Veterans Memorial in Washington, D.C., and environmental artworks such as the recent Confluence Project, a series of art installations along the Columbia River— Lin's design portfolio also includes museums, libraries, and residential projects.

Lin's contemporary house designs aspire to "the idea of simple," a serene minimalist vision that distills the economy, functionalism, and precision of Japanese, Scandinavian, Shaker, and early Modernist design. Lin's comparatively few residential projects, such as this Manhattan apartment designed in collaboration with New York architect David Hotson, make ingenious use of the simple box form to create the "calm, introspective spaces" she prefers. Lin's vacation home in the San Juan Mountains of Colorado and a house designed for a

LEFT: Walls and doors sheathed in blond sycamore veneer unpredictably slide open or pivot to reveal hidden rooms, puzzle box style.

FACING: The single bathroom space is transformed with a sliding wood panel into a two-bathroom configuration, and a shower enclosure is created with swiveling frosted-glass panels.

130

client in the same region also feature the box plan.

In this duplex renovation completed in 1998, Lin explores (and craftily explodes) rectangular planes and cubic volumes to get beyond the predictable box of Western architecture. The clean contemporary lines and minimalist décor of the design give it a deceptively simple appearance. This is a complex puzzle box of a house with more than meets the eye—secret tricks, spatial illusions, and hidden surprises.

Lin designed the witty architecture for an art collector and software entrepreneur who wanted to convert an uninspired 2,500-square-foot duplex into an intimate pied-à-terre to share with his wife and two children. For Lin, the limited space and sources of daylight and the awkward footprint of the original plan made the prospect less than ideal. To offset these limitations and turn the commission into an "ideal project," the client gave Lin carte blanche for the

renovation: no fixed budget, no fixed schedule, no specific design parameters, and no client intervention.

Given the freedom to plan the total design (from shell to furniture), Lin came up with a playful idea, inspired by Japanese design, for a flexible space responsive to the changing patterns of contemporary family life. "I envisioned a home that could fold in on itself, like origami or a transformer toy, changing its shape or function depending upon

how it was used." Lin's innovative solution owes much to the fluid art of Japanese house design, where volumes change shape through the use of screens and partitions, and the classic puzzle box. Interior volumes comprise boxes within boxes: transformable rooms with sliding panels and partitions and boxlike, shape-shifting furniture. "The design has a secretive and somewhat playful element, responding to my desire to give to the client a *smart* home

that works if one knows how to operate it," says Lin.

Entering the double doors from the fifth-floor apartment lobby, you step into a magical world of doubles and illusions. The staircase landing directly inside the entrance floats midway between a pair of ascending and descending stairs and figures as an intermediary plane between two realms. The stairs unfold, origami-like, in two directions—to the private upstairs level, with master suite

and guest rooms, and to the social downstairs level, with dining, living, and kitchen areas.

At first glance, the wall surfaces appear smooth, without any detectable openings or hidden panels. The blond sycamore walls and doors, consistently sheathed in four-inch-width veneer panels, unpredictably slide open or pivot to reveal hidden rooms, puzzle box style. The guest bedroom features a pivoting wardrobe on a track that slides out and

divides the room into two rooms. The master bedroom features an inner wall that slides away to reveal a workstation. The single bathroom space is transformed with a sliding wood panel into a two-bathroom configuration and a shower enclosure created with swiveling frosted-glass panels. The mechanisms that perform these magic tricks with walls and partitions are discretely concealed to give them an "outwardly simple appearance."

The finely crafted furniture, custom designed by Lin, shares this same precision, economy, and double—dual-purpose—identity. (The furniture design consumed almost eight months of the two-year project.) To use the furniture, you have to know the correct sequence of movements. The buffet opens up to reveal a dining table with chairs that fit inside like interlocking puzzle pieces or the components of robotic toys. Kitchen appliances are hidden behind the smooth

sycamore-surfaced cabinets. These compact, collapsible design elements generate space and create the illusion of lightness in the composition.

That illusion is furthered through the restrained palette of materials—sycamore paneling, maple floors, tile-scored concrete, and sandblasted glass. An aerial dynamic results from the sleek linear geometry of the blackened steel framework of the staircase, walls, and *shoji*-like doors. The rectilinear geometry is offset by

FACING FAR LEFT:
Sandblasted glass panels installed behind the staircase create a luminous backlit volume that gently lights the space.

FACING LEFT, AND RIGHT: The buffet opens to reveal a dining table with chairs that fit inside like interlocking puzzle pieces or the components of robotic toys.

curves in furniture and light fixtures. Translucent glass blurs spatial limits and brings ambient light into the interior. Glass panels installed behind the staircase rise the entire height of the duplex. The luminous skin of this backlit volume gently lights the space.

The result of this calm, balanced composition is an environment suited for quiet contemplation, a retreat from city life. The emphasis in Lin's design, however, leans toward the experiential and revela-tory, expressing her interest in the kinetic elements—movable pieces and moving people—of the composi-tion. Tranquility and stability counter an implicit dynamism in the subtly shifting hidden components of the design, pointing to Lin's interest in time in her work—not the static, "still moment" of architectonic space but "movement through space" and sequential puzzle-box revelation akin to the experience of traditional Japanese garden design.

133

VINTAGE DESIGN FOR THE WINE COUNTRY

METEOR VINEYARDS RESIDENCE

LOCATION: NAPA VALLEY, CALIFORNIA **ARCHITECT:** CUTLER ANDERSON ARCHITECTS

The dramatic symmetry and winged roof of the guesthouse give it an Asian aura.

Guided by a strong environmental ethic, Cutler Anderson Architects, on Bainbridge Island in Washington, designs architecture as "living art" connected with the natural world. Working on the leading edge of the Pacific Northwest tradition, the team of Jim Cutler and Bruce Anderson designs buildings to reveal "the nature and significance of the place and the nature and power of the materials." This design philosophy emphasizes native materials, regional vernacular, and bold functional expressiveness.

In the face of global climate changes, Cutler Anderson takes the Northwest tradition a step further in the direction of environmental stewardship. Jim Cutler believes it's important for architecture to support our "emotional connection to the living world." The firm has designed many award-winning public buildings and memorials, as well as significant residential architecture, including the Bill Gates compound on Lake Washington near Microsoft's Redmond Campus (a 40,000-square-foot lodge that took seven years to complete), and the spectacular Meteor Vineyards estate in the rolling hills of Napa Valley.

LEFT: The dramatic play of light in this interior corridor, a complex articulation of steel, rammed earth, and wood, speaks to the poetry of the design.

RIGHT: Symmetrically paired volumes and a prominent roof give the main pavilion a sense of grandeur reminiscent of Chinese architecture.

136

The owner of Meteor Vineyards, a new cabernet vintner, turned to Jim Cutler to design a family estate that would preserve the distinctive agricultural character of the Napa Valley region. The client and his wife wanted their home built close to the vineyards, with private outdoor areas for relaxation and a protected play area near the main house for their children. Cutler responded with a bold vibrant design that speaks the language of the wine country.

The plan for the architecture immerses the owners in the three zones of their twenty-seven-acre property: vineyard, meadow, and oak groves. An L-shaped axial design links three separate buildings. The 12,316-square-foot main house is sited between the meadow and the vineyard. A 1,200-square-foot guesthouse in the vineyard to the west is linked to the main house by a 130-foot bridge. A one-room studio is set in an oak grove at the end of

a 124-foot walkway on the opposite side of the house. The L-shape used for the arrangement of the architecture is repeated in the design of each structure. All three buildings feature L-shaped rammed-earth walls on the non-private vineyard side of the design, and wood frame and glass on the side facing the land.

The Meteor Vineyards project was Cutler Anderson's first experiment with ancient rammed-earth technology. Given the scale of the

Responding to, revealing, reflecting, and protecting the uniqueness of the real world around us should be our highest calling.

—Jim Cutler

137

project, they were looking for something massive that would give the architecture "a sense of solidity" and "place." And given the nature of the *terroir*—the soil, topography, and climate that give wine its distinctive qualities—constructing a building out of rammed earth was an appropriate solution. The walls and piers of the

architecture are made of the very soil that gives Napa Valley grapes their character (and cellars the wines to maturity). Cutler was very specific about the palette for the marbled volumes of rammed earth, experimenting with soil mixtures harvested from nearby Nunn's Canyon until he arrived at the desired shades. The

contractor was provided "veining" drawings to create the compacted marble layers of rammed earth.

Revealing the nature of materials is Cutler's way of honoring the earth and connecting buildings to their environment. Materials have a "will" to express their nature or spirit. "To anthropomorphize it, Arnold

139

In this wine region rain falls in three months of the year. The V-shaped roof featured on each building of the residence funnels precious rainwater into storage pools.

Schwarzenegger wouldn't want to insult Douglas fir by making cabinets [nonstructural elements] of the same material," says Cutler by way of illustration. Frank Lloyd Wright was also insistent that each material be used to express its ultimate purpose. Douglas fir was selected for the structure of the Meteor Vineyards residence; European steamed beech was chosen for the lighter finish. To enhance indoor-outdoor connection, rammed-earth piers are exposed on interior walls.

Principles of balance and symmetry underwrite the design. Wood-frame and glass elements effectively balance the rammed-earth elements of the composition. The massive volumes of the main pavilion are defined by a striking bilateral symmetry that lends the residence a sense of grandeur reminiscent of Chinese architecture. In that tradition, the principle of symmetry is applied to everything from palaces to farmhouses. Similarly, the guesthouse (with owl-eyed clerestory windows) is

divided into two volumes by a circulation corridor that leads from the vineyard through the guesthouse and across a footbridge to the pool terrace below the main house.

Symmetry characterizes the interior of the residence as well in both the private and public areas of the home. Rammed-earth piers and structural posts separate the open-flowing space of the informal kitchen-dining-living area. The composition of the formal dining room repeats that arrangement on a larger

LEFT: The symmetry and consistent palette of European steamed beech in this informal dining-living area create a soothing environment.

ABOVE: Structural posts separate the open-flowing space.

RIGHT: The composition of the formal dining room repeats the arrangement of the informal family dining area on a larger scale.

scale with a dramatic rammed-earth and steel fireplace.

Repetition gives unity to the complex labyrinth of the architecture. Throughout, larger-scaled design elements are repeated or "mimicked" on a smaller scale. Distinguishing features of the main house—rammed-earth volumes, cedar-shingled siding, window design, winged roofs—are repeated in the guesthouse. The V-shaped roof featured on all three buildings has a functional as well as an aesthetic value. In this wine region

where rain falls only three months of the year, the roofs are designed to funnel rainwater into storage pools, much in the way rainwater runs off of leaves to irrigate the soil. The architecture both mimics and poetically reveals the natural processes specific to vineyard life to express unity with its site. Mimicry of the vineyard at play in the design extends to the wood and steel-frame elements. Window frames and structural posts echo the horizontal and vertical rhythms of the rows of grapevines.

To enhance the connection with the outdoors from inside the interior of the residence, rammed-earth passages, wood-framed corridors, bridges, and walkways pick up the vineyard theme as well. Expansive glass windows throughout frame vineyard views. The way Cutler orchestrated these poetic effects to connect this new family of winegrowers with the land speaks to the deep respect for nature at the core of the design.

141

LOST TIMBERS, FOUND ARCHITECTURE

ISLAND RESIDENCE

LOCATION: PUGET SOUND, WASHINGTON **ARCHITECT:** CRAIG CURTIS, PRINCIPAL DESIGNER, MILLER/HULL PARTNERSHIP

ABOVE: This stately residence expresses regional character with rustic materials and a modern design that integrates the natural wooden landscape.

ABOVE RIGHT: The transparent volumes of the library and master suite virtually disappear into the natural surroundings.

The Miller/Hull Partnership of founding partners David Miller and Robert Hull, and architects Norm Strong and Craig Curtis, is committed to a "richer modernism" in its dynamic contribution to the Northwest architectural tradition. Since the inception of the firm in 1977, Miller/Hull has explored the development of two dominant themes in America's Western regional architecture: "the need to establish a defined place within the landscape," and "the art of rational building." A spare formal language that emphasizes lightness, transparency, and economy of means

distinguishes their work. Using efficient systems of building with revealed elements, their architecture is noted for its clarity and bold structural expressiveness.

For the entire history of the firm, Miller/Hull has designed environmentally sensitive buildings, beginning with award-winning earth-sheltered and solar designs. As leaders in green building, the partnership explores the use of recycled and salvaged materials. Recognized for innovative public architecture (community centers, higher-education facilities, and government offices), Miller/Hull also has

LEFT: From the master bedroom, a trestle leads to a private open-air deck with hot tub.

RIGHT: Wood paneling is used throughout the house in a combination of cherry and Douglas fir. Machiche is used for flooring in the kitchen, family, dining, and living rooms.

144

completed many residential projects ranging from affordable cabins to luxury homes.

This stately residence, sited on a steep bluff overlooking the Puget Sound and Olympic Mountains, expresses regional character with rustic materials and a modern design that integrates the natural wooded landscape. The owners asked Miller/Hull to design a residence for their family on a large parcel of forested land they had rescued from a plan to clear-cut and develop into a subdivision. This

private property is one of the only remaining pieces of land with extensive forests on the island. The owners challenged Craig Curtis, principal designer for the project, to preserve as much of the forest as possible and not cut down any significant trees. In the end, 95 percent of the trees on the property were saved. The private road that winds through the property's scenic terrain of meadows and mature forest to the residence was excavated without removing any trees. "It has the feeling of a National Park Service

road," says Curtis. "By the time you get to the house, you feel like you're in another world." The house is positioned in a clearing at the edge of the forest to fit within the existing trees.

The approximately 10,000-square-foot plan features three separate wings—the north wing, the main pavilion, and the south wing. The main pavilion, serving as the informal family space at the center of the house, features an open plan with dining, family, and kitchen areas. The pavilion is bracketed between

the gable-roofed two-story volumes of the north and south wings. The north wing includes a master suite, bedrooms, a library, a living room, a media room, and a recreation room. This wing cantilevers out to the west for dramatic southwest views from the glass-walled corners of the living room on the lower level and the master suite on the upper level. The architecture nestles into the edge of the forest of Douglas firs that towers more than a hundred feet. "The vertical piece of the house is closest to

the most significant trees," explains Curtis. The south wing at the edge of the clearing features a garage and a nanny/guest apartment.

The massive salvaged timbers that set the scale, mode, and tone for this seaworthy architecture commemorate a piece of Pacific maritime history. These timbers surfaced on Washington's coast after a long sea burial. Craig Curtis explains the story:

In 1921, a cargo ship carrying milled timbers from the Olympic Peninsula went down in a storm in Willapa Bay.

Just as the schematic design for this Miller/Hull project was underway, the hold of the submerged ship broke free and the timbers floated to the surface. The clients made a trip to examine the bounty firsthand. Impressed by the scale and condition of these timbers, the clients purchased fifteen of the best pieces and had them stored. These majestic timbers, some of them nearly forty feet long, became the inspiration for the design.

The timbers were planed into 19 x 19-inch columns and beams to form

LEFT: The Zen-spirited rock garden at the door and the "light totem" at the steps leading to the front entrance create a calm, vaguely Asian mood.

RIGHT: Two massive stone hearths interrupt the timbers and define areas for dining, family, and kitchen in the main pavilion.

146

cantilevered frames that create three open bays for the main pavilion.

To make the house fit into the forest, the owners requested cedar siding for the exterior. For a low profile, Miller/Hull developed a horizontal siding system using a combination of western red cedar and Alaskan yellow cedar for the pavilion structure and vertical western red cedar for gabled portions of the house. Curtis and the owners were grateful that it wasn't necessary to harvest this cedar from a healthy old-growth forest. Instead,

the entire western red cedar siding package was milled from a single stump—a thirty-foot-tall salvaged standing stump, several hundred years old, found by the owner on the Olympic Peninsula. "The milling technique chosen provided clear vertical grain finish, with a tightness and consistency of grain that is breathtakingly beautiful," says Curtis.

The approach to wood in the design essentially gives the exterior of the residence contrasting characters. The massive timber framework of the pavil-

ion expresses a robust rugged nature. The reserved front side of the house, by contrast, expresses a more refined nature with understated volumes smoothly wrapped with siding. The Zen-spirited rock garden at the door and the "light totem" at the steps leading to the front entrance create a calm, vaguely Asian mood. Curtis explains: "After decompressing from the drive through the forest, it was important to maintain a Zen-like quality as you approach the door." Smoothly clad with horizontal siding to match the exterior

façade, the front door visually dissolves into the adjacent walls.

Inside the residence, a spacious corridor flanked by timbers and naturally lit with skylights brings the forest into the home. That connection is furthered with two massive stone hearths that define areas for dining, family room, and kitchen. The living area flows seamlessly to the outside terrace and garden through expansive sliding glass doors. The openings are purposely overscaled to connect with the outdoors. "The bigger the opening, the

better the connection," observes Curtis, with reference to the great sliding doors of traditional Japanese buildings that inspired the design. Curtis noted strong parallels between the architectural traditions of the Pacific Northwest and Japan. Both aesthetics balance a contrast between "the wild and the tame" and emphasize the connection to the garden. Transitional space is key to an uninterrupted relationship between indoor and outdoor space. Curtis collaborated with landscape architect Tom Berger on the intuitive landscape

design for the residence. The terraced steps leading down to the garden express a monumental grandeur in conformity with the substantial character of the massive timbered pavilion.

The residence's architecture evokes an Asian sensibility with its prominent display of woods variously fashioned into timbered pergolas, deep eaves, and *engawa*-like decks. Yet in this Pacific Northwest context, those elements more strongly suggest the beams, decks, and galleys of a well-built ship.

REINVENTING THE
COUNTRY HOUSE

FURNITURE HOUSE NO. 5

LOCATION: SAGAPONACK, LONG ISLAND, NEW YORK **ARCHITECT:** SHIGERU BAN ARCHITECTS, TOKYO,
AND DEAN MALTZ, ASSOCIATE ARCHITECT, NEW YORK

ABOVE: The illuminated gallery of the interior corridor and the sculptural composition of porch terrace and pool rectangle provide a lesson in modern art.

ABOVE RIGHT: The cruciform plan of the Furniture House is based on van der Rohe's unbuilt Brick Country House: the four quadrants divide this house into public and private zones, each featuring an individual garden that integrates the interior with the flat wooded landscape.

International architect Shigeru Ban is highly acclaimed for his humorous and inventive approach to elegant design solutions. The primary objectives in his work are low-cost materials and the dissolution of boundaries between interior and exterior space. Ban's minimalist expressions take inspiration from the "skin and bones" architecture of Mies van der Rohe (father of the "less is more" principle), famous for his steel-enclosed glass volumes. The strong geometries and fluid space in Ban's work express his exploration of modernist ideas in fusion with the Japanese tradition. Ban's

iconic Curtain Wall House features two-story-high curtains along glass façades, almost in caricature of the transparency and flexibility of Japanese design.

Ban explores the use of alternative materials, giving new life and context to preexisting or banal materials such as paper. Paper is metamorphosed into pavilion spaces, sculptural installations, and innovative residential architecture. With the Paper Tube House—an inexpensive and durable housing unit made for the earthquake victims in Kobe, Japan—the traditional Asian house made of bamboo returns now made

of paper tubes. After Japan's 1995 earthquakes, when many lives were lost due to falling furniture, Ban began to explore the use of furniture as a primary structural component.

Furniture House No. 5 in Saga-ponack, New York, is Shigeru Ban's first house in this series built in the United States. The previous four were built in Japan and China (including one near the Great Wall of China). Ban was one of thirty-three mod-ernist architects invited to design a spec house at the Houses at

Sagaponack, a residential community on a hundred-acre wooded parcel of land in the Hamptons, a short drive from the ocean. The community of distinctive modernist houses was developed by The Brown Companies in association with architect Richard Meier to provide functional, moder-ately sized and priced single-family living spaces—essentially designed as an "anti-subdivision" to counter the trend of look-alike neo-traditional mansions built in the Hamptons dur-ing the 1980s and '90s.

Ban's Furniture House design marks a return to the playful spirit of the weekend escape houses designed in the Hamptons by modern archi-tects from the 1950s to the 1970s. These minimalist houses, with names like "Pin Wheel House" (Peter Blake), "Box Kite," and "Milk Carton" (Andrew Geller), were built as experiments in simple affordable design. The cruci-form plan of the Furniture House is based on van der Rohe's unbuilt Brick Country House (1924): the four quad-rants divide this house into public

and private zones, each featuring an individual garden that integrates the interior with the flat wooded landscape. The 3,700-square-foot space includes an open living-dining area, four bedrooms, four bathrooms, pool and covered porch area, and a gallery.

The Furniture House is composed of eighty prefabricated building components that integrate its open interior and exterior space. Ban's innovative approach is a reinterpretation of the inexpensive and time-efficient mass production advocated in early modernism. The Furniture House was conceived with the understanding that architectural standardization can lead to "spatial elasticity."

These modular furniture units, made out of plywood with a maple veneer, provide the structural system and spatial division of the house while also providing extensive storage. There are ten different unit types, ranging from wardrobe cabinets to bookcases to garden storage cabinets. Each has a standard measurement depending upon whether it serves as

FACING: With its flat slab roof and sleek minimalist volumes, the Furniture House resembles an abstract modern sculpture.

ABOVE: The main living area features five floor-to-ceiling glass doors that slide open on steel tracks for total connection with the outdoors.

151

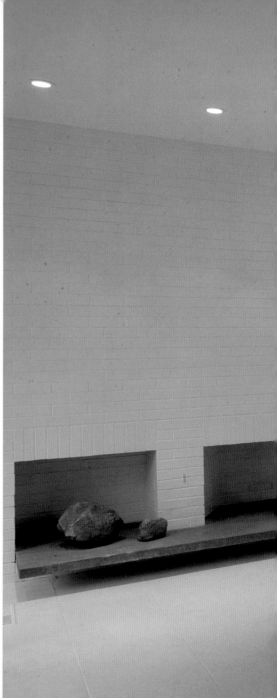

a box or a panel, an exterior or interior unit. With this ingenious system, several workers can install them in a day once the units are delivered to the site, reducing labor time and construction costs. Ban chose the prefabricated Furniture House idea for the Sagaponack project to reduce costs because the remote (from Japan) location would prevent him from supervising the construction.

As with the traditional Japanese house, flexibly designed to respond to the weather, the views, and the moods of its inhabitants (with sliding screens), the Furniture House is equipped for a flexible relationship with its environment. The main living area features five floor-to-ceiling glass doors that slide open on steel tracks for a full-on view of the woods, providing a sense of flowing space with no division between the interior and the surrounding land-scape. The austere modern museum character of the interior, with its low-key palette and clean abstract lines, minimizes the presence of the architecture and draws attention to framed views of the outdoors. The kitchen area flowing from the main living space is casually separated with an Asian-themed screen con-structed of paper tubes.

In the spirit of modernism and the modern museum, the house fea-tures a long gallery adjacent to the pool area that provides wall space for displaying paintings. The gallery doubles as a glass-walled corridor connecting to the main living area of the home.

Ban effectively promotes transparency (dissolves interior-exterior boundaries) in the design by utilizing the same structural furniture components inside and out. With their simple functional nature and uniform veneer, the furniture units exert a minimal presence, allowing for a sense of expansiveness and spatial flow beyond the limits of the actual square footage of the home.

The connection with the outdoors is furthered in the design by extending the furniture units in three horizontal axes from the house structure out into the landscape. Rhythmically spaced columns of furniture units line up to form a portico that leads from the carport to the main entrance and to radiate in lintel-capped colonnades from the core of the house. With its flat slab roof and sleek minimalist volumes, the Furniture House resembles an abstract modern sculpture. This functional-but-elegant design effectively blurs the distinction between art, craft, and high technology.

FACING: This minimalist partition reminiscent of an Asian screen is made of paper tubes. It separates the kitchen zone while affording glimpses of the space beyond.

ABOVE: The austere modern museum character of the interior minimizes the presence of the architecture and draws attention to framed views of the landscape.

153

154   The most efficient systems are the simplest. My basic philosophy

has always been to build a house that improves the environment

instead of compromising it. I want to help people ground back

into the earth, into nature.

—Tony Gwilliam

HOUSES TO GO: ASIAN TAKEOUTS

THE POST-AND-BEAM CONSTRUCTION of traditional Asian houses makes them quite versatile. These timber-frame structures are built with precut parts ready to assemble on-site or to dismantle and carry out to a different location. This chapter features Asian-inspired timber-frame products developed by innovative companies offering houses made with prefabricated modular components, or "kits"—The Bali T-House developed by Tony Gwilliam, The Minahasa House of Carey Smoot, Source Tropical, the Rikyu prototype developed by Paul Discoe, Joinery Structures, and the Haiku House produced by Charla Honea.

These high-quality "houses-to-go" are rewriting the definition of kit houses. Besides the strong aesthetic appeal of these Asian-inspired designs, their modular systems give them wide flexibility with floor plans. As these designs illustrate, prefabrication does not limit the homeowner to generic and identical results. Their affordability and durability make them further attractive. Committed to earth-friendly design, these companies build their products with natural, nontoxic, and reused wood materials.

DOING MORE WITH LESS: THE BALI T-HOUSE

YOGA PAVILION

LOCATION: SANTA BARBARA, CALIFORNIA **ARCHITECT:** TONY GWILLIAM

Whilst traveling in Bali, I often found myself staying in simple pavilions amongst the rice fields. I felt happy there, protected from the sun and rain yet connected to the universe around me. . . . One day in 1996, this brilliant-yet-simple T-house design came to me and the first T-house was soon handcrafted in Ojai, California, later to be followed by others back in Indonesia, its birthplace.

—Tony Gwilliam

ABOVE: Gwilliam's T-house design celebrates Bali's colorful fusion of Hindu and Buddhist traditions.

ABOVE RIGHT: This simple *bale* (pavilion) provides a versatile retreat for meditation, tea time, or relaxation.

International architect Tony Gwilliam, "design outlaw" on the ecological frontier, worked alongside Buckminster Fuller in the geodesic dome industry before envisioning his own design for earth-friendly shelter. With Fuller, Gwilliam developed and manufactured the lightweight high-tensile aluminum and silicon dome structure as an efficient and economical alternative to traditional Western housing. While the building boom surged in the 1980s and '90s, launching wide-scale production of houses with astronomical footprints constructed with toxic build-

ing materials (from particleboard to PVC), Gwilliam continued to champion the cause of the housing industry's underdog—the environmentally sensitive small-scale house.

In the pioneering spirit of Fuller's dome or Ford's Model T, Gwilliam designed a prototype to improve the quality of life—the T-house. For years, Gwilliam had sketched ideas for a simple structure, "a space for conscious living." At last he came up with the T-house design. Gwilliam's design concept swaps Fuller's futuristic "autonomous dwelling machine" for an

interdependent "living systems" model inspired by traditional Asian architecture—the *bale*, the pavilion structure in Indonesian compounds (Balinese families do not live in a "house" in the Western sense, but a compound with separate pavilions), and the Japanese teahouse, as the name T-house implies.

Built on a humble scale with simple rustic materials, the T-house is designed to work *with* nature, as in Asian tradition. Western architecture

traditionally "fights against nature and the outside," observes Gwilliam. Asian design encourages harmonious balance between the architecture and the natural world, and is outward oriented—open to nature—rather than inward oriented.

Though not intended for mass production—the T-house is geared for small eco-village or resort development in tropical regions—the design's modular kit-system construction makes it versatile and affordable.

Crafted in sustainable natural materials—ironwood, alang alang, and bamboo—harvested from forests in Indonesia, the T-house is also good for the earth. Gwilliam's design models environmental stewardship with its small footprint. "One point I wish to emphasize is the importance of small when it comes to ecological design," says Gwilliam.

If you are building a McMansion, even with green materials, the energy both for building and in use is immoral,

FACING: This Bali T room provides a poolside painting studio and retreat.

RIGHT: A classic Balinese woven-bamboo design was selected for the ceiling.

whereas if good materials are used well to fit their characteristics, then sometimes a more exotic material may be more suited for the job. . . . It's a matter of choosing the best fit. We use ironwood for our houses because it is very strong and durable, providing a long-lived house, very resistant to rot and insects. It may be disassembled and moved, modified, bought and sold, and remodeled, but the structure will provide a family home for at least 100 years, and after that, much of the wood will be reused in other ways before composting and completing the cycle.

As an experiment in "minimalist impact living," Gwilliam and his partner, Marita Vidal, an architect from Argentina, developed the pilot project Bali T in the Rice—a village of T-houses located on a rice plantation near Lodtundah. The success of this project spawned a second eco-village near Ubud, in central Bali, and has attracted an export market in the tropical resort industry. Gwilliam plans to introduce his ecological village concept in other Indonesian countries and as far as Cambodia, where he will teach people how to build these economical nontoxic houses for their communities.

The T-house aesthetic appeals to the "connoisseur of the simple"— those who appreciate the economy and elegance of its minimalist proportions as well as the sensual beauty of its handcrafted materials.

"The house is more like a beautiful wooden bowl or a piece of furniture than a building," says Gwilliam. One of the most complete and authentic Bali T-houses designed and built in the United States is this charming yoga pavilion perched, birdlike, over a Japanese water garden at a private residence in Santa Barbara.

The owner, a documentary film-maker, learned about Bali T-houses from a friend and contacted Tony Gwilliam to create a garden sanctu-ary for her in a sheltered wooded area behind her residence. The natural landscape in that part of the property, shaded with fragrant cedars, lends itself to the "deep environment of peace" provided by the design.

T-house architecture features versatile kit-system construction with modular components that can be variously configured to suit a client's needs. Depending on design prefer-ences and program, the modules can be vertically stacked into a two-story structure or expanded horizontally into a compound-style arrangement, as in many traditional Balinese vil-lages. This yoga pavilion features a one-module, single-story plan. Its structural components were crafted in Bali, precut according to the prescribed footprint (specially engi-neered for California code require-ments), and shipped in a twenty-foot container to the site. A local con-tractor and a crew of four workers

assembled and erected the pavilion in less than two weeks.

Like most Bali T structures, the yoga pavilion was constructed with plantation-grown ironwood, a dense tropical hardwood resistant to termites that lasts over a hundred years. The graceful shingled roof was based on a Balinese thatched-roof design. The timber-frame (post-and-beam) components were assembled with traditional pegged joints, with the structural pillars anchored into concrete piers. The materials are used efficiently in the construction process due to the precise measurements required of joinery, where every millimeter counts.

The pavilion's simple interior reflects the influence of Japanese house design, where wood itself is the primary element of the décor and space is fluidly partitioned with flexible components—removable screens and blinds, futons, and floor cushions—to maximize limited space

ABOVE LEFT: Traditional Japanese-teahouse garden design inspired the intimate water garden for this T-house.

ABOVE: The pavilion projects over a lily pond to heighten the connection with the sensual pleasures of the natural environment.

163

and open the interior to nature. The interior can be configured for dining or sleeping arrangements: the center floor panel lifts up and transforms into a *kotatsu* (a low wooden table with a heater underneath). Ironwood and glass pocket doors, with a grid pattern reminiscent of traditional *shoji* (paper screen), slide away for an open-air experience. Traditional Japanese teahouse garden design inspired the intimate water garden. The pavilion projects over a koi pond

to heighten the connection with the garden and the sensual pleasures of the natural environment.

The owner enjoys the peace and beauty of this garden retreat for her yoga practice. The pavilion also provides a delightful space for small social gatherings. Soon after the yoga pavilion was built, the owner was married there and held a wedding reception in the garden.

ABOVE: The structural pillars of the pavilion are anchored into concrete piers.

FACING ABOVE: The pavilion's simple and versatile interior reflects the influence of Japanese house design. A center floor panel lifts up and transforms into a *kotatsu* table.

FACING: The elegant ceiling is crafted with woven bamboo.

TALES FROM THE SPICE TRADE

MINAHASA HOUSE

LOCATION: OAHU, HAWAII **ARCHITECTURAL DESIGNER:** CAREY SMOOT, SOURCE TROPICAL

ABOVE: The original Minahasa house prototype, Tomohan, North Sulawesi. The structure was later built on the big island of Hawaii.

ABOVE RIGHT: This two-story Minahasa model was shipped to Kauai, Hawaii. Pictured here are the Minahasa siding and second-floor posts, which Source Tropical provides carved. Left open, the lower level could serve as a garage, storage, and washroom area.

Architectural designer Carey Smoot founded the design company Source Tropical (1991) to make tropical materials available in the Hawaiian Islands. The company expanded to design, fabricate, and import precut houses and bamboo furniture. Exporting these Indonesian products to Hawaii, Smoot makes a point of preserving a sense of place: "I don't bring Bali to Hawaii." Rather, he specializes in designing architecture with regional character that emphasizes "connection with place."

The Minahasa is a precut tropical-style house fabricated from chempaka wood, a tropical hardwood from Indonesia. Smoot developed the Minahasa prototype from extensive research of indigenous tropical island architecture. In the 1980s, Smoot leased 8,000 acres in Indonesia to grow tropical hardwoods and fabricate reproductions of native designs from Fiji, Yap Island, and Sulawesi in a factory in North Sulawesi. "I had access to the materials, which was a big factor in producing my vision," Smoot explains.

The name "Minahasa" comes from the indigenous people of North Sulawesi and their distinctive architecture. The

European elements of their typical houses—French windows, hip-and-gable roof, and decorative railings—are unique to this province. In his research of native architecture, Smoot found this Sulawesi design to be the only European-influenced architecture in Indonesia. Its mixed lineage is indebted to Dutch settlement in North Sulawesi during the Spice Trade era of the 1700s. Dutch sailors took a wrong turn and ended up in Sulawesi, north of the coveted "Spice Islands." Smoot selected the Dutch-influenced Minahasa design for his kit-house prototype, as he perceived that a tropical style with a European flavor would appeal to a Western market.

The standard shell of the two-level Minahasa features an open ground floor with structural posts and an enclosed second-floor bedroom area. An open wood-sheathed ceiling extends over the living and dining areas. The Minahasa is easily assembled from factory-processed, modular-systems-kit components crafted of chempaka, a durable hardwood resistant to mildew and termites. Optional roof coverings include thatch, ironwood shingles, and recycled corrugated metal. The Minahasa is economical to build and can be designed and engineered to serve as a simple vacation retreat or a multistructure compound. The highly flexible structure is adaptable to sites with

FAR LEFT: The French windows, hip-and-gable roof, and decorative features of the Minahasa house design are indebted to the history of Dutch settlement in North Sulawesi.

LEFT: A code system is used for framing the roof trusses. Note that chempaka has no knots. The roof deck was 3/4-inch plywood with a woven bamboo finished ceiling to give it a tropical look. The framing was done on the ground and then dismantled and packed in a shipping container.

BELOW: Carey Smoot's first prototype was produced at his factory in Tomohan, North Sulawesi, in 1991. Smoot modified the traditional Minahasa design by building a larger overhang and a steeper pitched roof with a gable vent. Most future clients chose the ironwood-shingle roof option over the corrugated metal roof pictured here.

challenging topography making it effective in steep hillside locations.

The Minahasa house built in Kauai, Hawaii, was originally planned by its owners to serve as a small house for a caretaker's residence, with a shop and utility space on the lower level. For the owners themselves, Smoot had designed a compound with four pavilion-style buildings. Smoot suggested that his clients economize by making use of precut buildings from Indonesia similar to the kit-house structure planned for their caretaker. Smoot explains, "Once the building was delivered, the owners chose to convert it into their home and kick the caretaker out!" The Minahasa design was modified from the standard model when the owners decided to live there full time. They added dormers and a deck that wraps around the building's exterior to enjoy the views. "They never built the grand design, which was stunning on the site, 350 feet from the beach on a hillside with great breezes and views. But they are happy, which is the crux of good master plan design."

169

MINKA MEETS BAUHAUS

HERSEY RESIDENCE

LOCATION: MILLBROOK, NEW YORK **ARCHITECT:** HAIKU HOUSES, INC., AND
HIRO CONSTRUCT, JOHN HERSEY DESIGNER

ABOVE: Hersey's modernist departure from the standard Haiku House design wraps one side of the house in glass. The reflections of the forest give the house a minimalist presence and connect it with its surroundings.

ABOVE RIGHT: Hersey redesigned the standard Haiku House kit to suit his modernist vision.

Soon after reviewing architect's plans for a contemporary house he planned to build on a woodsy site in the Hudson River Valley, artist John Hersey sat down for lunch with a friend. That meeting was serendipitous. Hersey learned about an attractive and more cost-efficient alternative—Haiku Houses. This company specializes in manufacturing a systems-built modular "kit" version of the traditional sixteenth-century Japanese country house. Most of the houses built in Millbrook, New York, these days are replicas of eighteenth-century farmhouses. Hersey was drawn to the Japanese farmhouse as a contemporary rural house alternative.

Hersey explained that he wasn't interested in a Japanese house per se so much as the structural clarity and simplicity of the design. "The essence of the structure is so pure and simple, but so strong at the same time," says Hersey. As an artist, with a Yale degree in architecture and family roots in Asia, that aesthetic sensibility is in his blood: "My father, the author of *Hiroshima*, was born in Tsinsen, China, and I grew up with an Asian bent."

To research the Haiku Houses alternative, Hersey went to visit Charla Honea, owner of the company, in Nashville, Tennessee. Charla herself lives in a Haiku House. (Interestingly, during the construction of her house, Charla and her husband decided to purchase the company that built it.) Hersey turned down the standard "soups and nuts" package in favor of a more American interpretation of the Japanese country house produced by Haiku Houses.

The house John Hersey designed with the Haiku Houses product is a melding of Asian and American influences. As Hersey humorously describes it, "I put Japanese design on steroids." Hersey made no apology for taking liberties with the traditional design. "Americans always blow things up. Contemporary Japanese design has little to do with sixteenth-century farmhouses, either, yet is minimalist and contemporary." Hersey continues, "As

an artist, I've lived in many industrial spaces. Subconsciously, I was trying to re-create an urban space in a rural area." If you had to put a style label on it, Hersey says you might call it "urban rustic."

Charla Honea remarked that Haiku Houses had never before built a house as modern as this one. For Hersey's design modifications, the company had to reengineer the frame. Major departures from the standard model included substituting

The Haiku House design recalls the classic seventeenth-century farmhouses built in Japanese snow country.

an entire wall of sliding glass doors and breaking up the grand veranda encircling the house. In addition, the exterior walls were moved outside of the structural columns to maximize interior space. Approximately half of the house was built on ground level over a foundation while the rest is elevated on poles like a tree house. With an open and fluid floor plan, the ceiling structure above is exposed throughout, modeled after the classic *minka* (Japanese folk house) with

a sixteen-foot skylight at the apex. Walls connect with structure halfway to the ceiling. The plan features 3,700 square feet of living space on the main level with a large, open living room that flows into a kitchen-dining area, and a private area with a library, two bedrooms, and two baths. A 2,000-square-foot basement features an in-house studio with a darkroom and etching press.

Each Haiku House is custom crafted to give the feeling of a com-

pletely handmade structure. Douglas fir poles are lathe turned and sanded, notched, drilled, and given a protective coating. Each beam is shaped and cut to the precise requirements of the client to assure quality as well as ease and speed of assembly. The Douglas fir frame for the Hersey residence was precisely cut at a mill in British Columbia, numbered, crated, and shipped 3,000 miles across the country to Hersey's site. The frame was delivered in

173

LEFT: The graceful interior glows with lustrous natural woods.

FACING ABOVE: The exposed joinery of traditional post-and-beam construction gives the residence an earthy character.

FACING BELOW: The beauty of the bones. "I love the purity and simplicity of the structural system," says Hersey.

two truckloads—first the girders and floor joists, followed by the roof structure. Hersey employed a crew of highly skilled craftsmen—local barn builders—to assemble the complex joinery system.

As general contractor with his company Hiro Construct, Hersey was on-site to witness the entire process of building "Dolphin House" (a name evolved from a series of sailboats), from the excavation of the foundation to the delivery of the truckloads of

timber-frame parts to the assembly of the joinery structure meticulously crafted in the traditional style—with the exception of steel bolts added for strength, and a crane to hoist the heavy Douglas fir timbers into position. "I love the purity and simplicity of the structural system," Hersey comments. "To be able to put up a whole roof without building one wall is exquisite. . . . It's sort of in the Buckminster Fuller category with a rural character."

Jaded by the pretenses of Western architecture, Hersey appreciates the beauty of the simple, functional architecture of his Haiku House. "After so many centuries of ornaments, it's hard to peel it back to something so beautiful and essential in its own right."

with Japanese design elements built with recycled and salvaged urban materials. The company developed the Rikyu prototype in 2006—an economical kit-system design with modular components based on the Japanese *ken* (module) translated to Western measurement. Discoe explains,

After spending a decade building the Woodside project, an intense project in which we invented new building solutions to the many complex challenges we faced with each structure, I wanted to work on something more modest. *The idea of shop-built, precut houses is an ancient idea in Japan. In many cases, pieces of a house are constructed in one location and assembled on-site. With the kit of parts, we are modernizing an old idea.*

The parts of the prefabricated modular kits are produced at the Joinery Structures workshop. Each kit contains a complete set of posts, beams, panels, ceiling pieces, and stair layout. Parts are assembled using Japanese joinery construction, but the process has been simplified and standardized for Western measurements to reduce labor and cost. To suit client preferences, the parts can be arranged in an infinite number of ways, and the kits can be designed for a large or small footprint.

The objective for each complete kit of parts, once installed on its site, is to express a nondualistic relationship between people and their environment. In Discoe's practice, this means "working together with the elements to create a space that is conducive to a peaceful, balanced life."

LEFT: The design for the guesthouse unit is based on standardized 8 x 8-foot modular components. This small structure echoes the Asian profiles of the main house.

RIGHT: The wide verandas of the main dwelling, crafted in Monterey cypress, expand the space of the home and connect it with the wooded landscape.

Live Edge constructed its first Rikyu kit-of-parts house in northern Sonoma County, California, in 2007—a one-bedroom guesthouse unit designed to accompany the custom-designed "main dwelling" built for the clients by Joinery Structures. The main house expresses the Asian profiles and modular timber-frame construction of the smaller unit but includes custom features beyond the standard items offered in the prefab package.

The three-bedroom house comprises forty-two (8 x 8-foot) modules, or about 2,600 square feet, including decks and exterior balcony. Reclaimed materials used for building the structure include Douglas fir for the frame, redwood for the doors and windows, Monterey cypress for the decks and cabinetry, and madrone flooring (a by-product of the forest industry). The 860-square-foot guesthouse structure features horizontal timbers crafted in reclaimed and remanufactured Douglas fir, bamboo flooring, and doors, decking, and cabinetry in a combination of wood salvaged from the urban forest. The simple corrugated metal roof is painted with black tar. With its economical and sustainable materials, simple lines, and easy assembly, the Rikyu prefab design provides an elegant solution for basic shelter. It's the way of the future.

More projects are in the works. The structures utilize reused, non-toxic, economical materials that are easy to assemble for basic shelter. It's the way of the future.

Sources

Bean, Cathy Bao. *The Chopsticks-Fork Principle: A Memoir and Manual.* Allamuchy, New Jersey: We Press, 2002.

Bender, Tom. *Building with the Breath of Life.* Manzanita, Oregon: Fire River Press, 2000.

———. *Silence, Song and Shadows: Our Need for the Sacred in Our Surroundings.* Manzanita, Oregon: Fire River Press, 2000.

Berliner, Nancy. *Yin Yu Tang: The Architecture and Daily Life of a Chinese House.* Boston: Tuttle Publishing, 2003.

Black, Alexandra. *The Japanese House: Architecture and Interiors.* Boston: Tuttle Publishing, 2000.

Clodagh. *Total Design: Contemplate, Cleanse, Clarify, and Create Your Personal Spaces.* New York: Random House, 2001.

Frank, Ann Wall. *Northwest Style: Interior Design and Architecture in the Pacific Northwest.* San Francisco: Chronicle Books, 1999.

Helmi, Rio, and Barbara Walker. *Bali Style.* New York: The Vendome Press, 1995.

Itoh, Teiji. *Traditional Domestic Architecture of Japan.* New York: Weatherhill, 1972.

Kakuzo, Okakura. *The Book of Tea.* Rutland, Vermont: Charles E. Tuttle Company, 1956.

Koren, Leonard. *Wabi-Sabi for Artists, Designers, Poets & Philosophers.* Berkeley: Stone Bridge Press, 1994.

Lin, Maya. *Boundaries.* New York: Simon and Schuster, 2000.

McQuaid, Matilda. *Shigeru Ban.* New York: Phaidon Press Inc., 2003.

Nakashima, George. *The Soul of the Tree: A Woodworker's Reflections.* Tokyo: Kodansha International, 1981.

Olson, Sheri. *Miller/Hull: Architects of the Pacific Northwest.* New York: Princeton Architectural Press, 2001.

———. *Cutler Anderson Architects.* Gloucester, Massachusetts: Rockport Publishers, 2004.

Ostergard, Derek. *George Nakashima: Full Circle.* New York: Weidenfeld & Nicolson, 1989.

Pfeiffer, Bruce Brooks. *Frank Lloyd Wright: Masterworks.* New York: Rizzoli, 1993.

Rao, Peggy Landers. *Nature on View: Homes and Gardens Inspired by Japan.* New York: Weatherhill, 1993.

Rao, Peggy Landers, and Len Brackett. *Building the Japanese House Today.* New York: Harry N. Abrams, 2005.

Takishita, Yoshihiro. *Japanese Country Style.* Tokyo: Kodansha International, 2002.

Treib, Marc, and Ron Herman. *A Guide to The Gardens of Kyoto.* Toyko: Kodansha International, 2003.

Wright, Frank Lloyd. *The Natural House.* New York: Horizon Press, 1954.

Zelov, Chris, editor. *Design Outlaws on the Ecological Frontier.* New York: Knossus Publishing, 1997.

Photo Credits

Art Grice: 9 (right); 75; 94–99; 134–39; 140 (left)

Aya Brackett: 16–29

Bennett Bean: 113, 117

Bill Taylor: 54–55; 183

Carey Smoot: 166–69

Chris Marona: 15; 53; 36–43; 60–65

Eric Schiller, courtesy of Maya Lin Studio: 128–29, 131, 132 (right), 133

Gary Braasch: 78 (above left)

John Hersey: 170–75

John Stillman, Courtesy of Peacock & Lewis, Architects: 118–23

Kay Wettstein: 148–53

Michael Mathers: 76–79

Nic Lehoux: 2–3; 127; 142–47

Olivier Koning: 86–93

Paul Warhol, courtesy of Maya Lin Studio: 130–32 (left)

Photography courtesy Houses at Sagaponack, 149 (isometric, right)

Photography courtesy Ki Arts, Inc.: 30–35

Photography courtesy of Sotheby's New York (Auction Catalog, December 2006, New Life for the Noble Tree, The Dr. Arthur & Evelyn Krosnick Collection of Masterworks by George Nakashima): 56–59

Ric Noyle: 66–71

Richard Van Den Berg: 44–49; 45 (drawing)

Roslyn Banish: 176–78

Sharon Risedorph: 141

Todd Mason: 111–12, 114–16

Tom Bender: 80–85

Tony Gwilliam: 157–65

Resources

Beck Studio
Architectural Design
1326 Fifth Avenue, Suite 348
Seattle, WA 98101
206.749.9286
inquiry@beckstudio.net

The Berger Partnership
Landscape Architecture
1721 – 8th Avenue North
Seattle, WA 98109
206.325.6877
info@bergerpartnership.com

Clodagh Design
Architecture and Interior Design
670 Broadway, 4th Floor
New York, NY 10012
212.780.5755
info@clodagh.com

Cutler Anderson Architects
Architectural Design
135 Parfitt Way SW
Bainbridge Island, WA 98110
206.842.4710
contact@cutler-anderson.com

Reveal Designs
Home Products
711 Westchester Avenue, Suite 2
White Plains, NY 10604
914.220.0277

East Wind (Higashi Kaze)
*Traditional Japanese Architecture,
Design and Woodworking*
21020 Shields Camp Road
Nevada City, CA 95959
530.265.3744
mail@eastwindinc.com

Haiku Houses
*Country Houses of Sixteenth-
Century Japan*
P.O. Box 1151
Franklin, TN 37065
615.673.9024
www.haikuhouses.com

Joinery Structures
Traditional Asian Timber-Frame
Design/Build
2500 Kirkham Street
Oakland, CA 94607
510.451.6345
js@joinerystructures.com

Joseph Lancor Architects
1276 Mokulua Drive
Kailua, HI 96734
808.261.6610
lancorj001@hawaii.rr.com

Ki Arts
Traditional Japanese Woodworking
P.O. Box 631
Occidental, CA 95465
707.874.3361
info@kiarts.com

Maya Lin Studio
*Architecture and Environmental
Design*
112 Prince Street
New York, NY 10012
212.941.6463
mlinstudio@aol.com

Michael Fuller Architects
710 East Durant Avenue
Aspen, CO 81611
970.925.3021
contact@mfullerarchitects.com

The Miller/Hull Partnership
Polson Building
71 Columbia, Sixth Floor
Seattle, WA 98104
206.682.6837
www.millerhull.com

**Shigeru Ban Architects and Dean
Maltz Architect**
330 West 38th Street, Suite 811
New York, NY 10018
212.925.2211
contact@dma-ny.com
Tokyo@ShigeruBanArchitects.com

Source Tropical
*Elements and Services,
Authentic designs influenced by
Asian and Pacific cultures*
Indonesia:
Jalan Sekuta, Gang Orchid #8
Sanur, Denpassar
Bali, Indonesia 80288a
62.361.289332

Hawaii:
46-148 Kahuhipa Street
Kaneohe, HI 96744
www.sourcetropical.com

Tom Bender Architect
Ecological Design
38755 Reed Road
Nehalem, OR 97131
503.368.6294
tbender@nehalemtel.net

Tommy Hein Architects
100 South Oak Street
Telluride, CO 81435
970.728.1220
www.tommyhein.com

Tony Gwilliam Architect
T House
United States:
P.O. Box 1235
Ojai, CA 93024
805.646.7355

Indonesia:
P.O. Box 3962
Ubud 80571
Bali, Indonesia
BaliTHouses@yahoo.com

Nakashima Studios
Custom Furniture Design
1847 Aquetong Road
New Hope, PA 18938
215.862.2272

Peacock & Lewis Architects and Planners, Inc.
11760 U.S. Highway One, Suite 102
North Palm Beach, FL 33408
561.626.9704
www.peacockandlewis.com

Wu Way Landscaping
James Pyle Company
15450 Lakeview Drive
Grass Valley, CA 95945
530.273.5397